Night Conversations with Cardinal Martini

The Relevance of the Church for Tomorrow

Cardinal Carlo M. Martini
and Georg Sporschill

Paulist Press
New York / Mahwah, NJ

Originally published as: Carlo M. Martini / Georg Sporschill, *Jerusalemer Nachtgespräche*. Über das Risiko des Glaubens © 2010 5th edition Verlag Herder GmbH, Freiburg im Breisgau

Translated from the German by Lorna Henry

Library of Congress Control Number: 2012949216

ISBN 978-0-8091-4799-1

Published by Paulist Press
997 Macarthur Boulevard
Mahwah, New Jersey 07430

www.paulistpress.com

Printed and bound in the
United States of America

Contents

Foreword One v

Foreword Two vii

1. What Sustains Life? 1

2. Courage to Decide..33

3. Making Friends 51

4. Being Close to God 77

5. Learning to Love 89

6. For an Open Church..101

7. Fighting Against Injustice..119

Foreword One

A woman from Vienna with whom I have been in contact for several years told me many times about Father Georg Sporschill. For a long time she has been supporting his work for street children in Romania and Moldavia.

I was pleased when I heard that Father Georg was coming to Jerusalem. I had heard a lot about him as a pastor for young people and wanted to know more about him and his work. I already knew of one of his books: *My Problem: Karl Rahner Answers Young People*.

He had encouraged young people to formulate their questions in a letter to Karl Rahner, and out of that came this interesting book.

In Jerusalem we talked a lot about today's youth, often late into the night—although I'm a morning person. We let our minds dream. At night, ideas come more readily than in the sober light of day. What does youth expect? And what does the world expect of its youth? A difficult world demands their involvement.

This little book came out of those night conversations. The most important parts are the questions from the young people. Are they still interested enough today to criticize us, the Church, the establishment? Or are they moving away without a word? I am convinced that where there are conflicts, a fire is burning, and there the Holy Spirit is at work. I have seen that by meeting with many young people.

Everything is a gift. When I was a child, four or five years old, my mother took me to a beauty contest. We all stood in a line. On the command we were to start running. It was not only good looks but also movement that was being judged. I didn't hear the call of the leader and remained standing on the spot when all the rest took off. Then the leader came up to me and put me in first place.

This story from my childhood seems to me an image for my life. I have not heard some calls, or not taken notice of them. In spite of this, the Jesuit order made me Rector of the Pontifical Biblical Institute in Rome. Jesuits were not meant to be bishops, and certainly not someone from Turin in Milan, and yet the Pope called me there to be archbishop. Truly I can say together with the words of Wisdom, "I exerted little effort and found much peace." Life has shown me that God is good. He never ceases to seek our help for a more peaceful world.

This book has been written in tandem. Both of us, Father Georg and I, are responsible for it all. The careful reader will quickly see that some pages reflect the experience of Cardinal Martini, while others correspond more to the many contacts made by Father Georg with young people at home and abroad.

Now this little book has passed out of our hands. These are thoughts that are dear to both of us. Many conversations with the youngsters have moved us. With them we experienced an open church. They are fighting against injustice and want to learn about love. They give hope to a difficult world.

Cardinal Carlo M. Martini, SJ
Jerusalem, November 2007

Foreword Two

I used to sit under a palm tree in the garden of the Pontifical Biblical Institute in Jerusalem while writing *Bimails* with Wolfgang Feneberg and Ruth Zenkert. *Bimails* are biblical teachings for leaders. During that time I would meet Cardinal Martini each day. He was interested in my work with street children. And so we became friends.

Cardinal Carlo Maria Martini is a Jesuit. From 1980 until 2002 he was Archbishop of Milan, the largest diocese in the world. He bore this responsibility the same length of time as Ambrose, the great bishop who brought peace to Milan in the fourth century. At seventy-five, Cardinal Martini relinquished his office to his successor and exchanged the Archbishop's palace in Milan for a simple room in the Jesuit House in Jerusalem, the city of his "first love." He lives here with students from around the world. Many come in order to practice the Ignatian exercises with him, to thank him and to seek his advice. "I want to pray for the Church and for my diocese. That is my work today," says the Cardinal. I don't know whether he has much time now for the biblical languages he wanted to study again.

Cardinal Martini was considered for many years as *papabilis,* a candidate for Pope. The fact that he has Parkinson's disease may have been a factor against him. The media in Italy often try to portray the courageous Cardinal as *Anti-Papa*, against the Pope, because of his openness. The Cardinal's response is to smile and say: "Rather I am *Ante-Papa,* a precursor and preparer for the Holy Father." Indeed, Pope Benedict XVI asked him to launch his book *Jesus of Nazareth* in Paris. The Pope's book is a testimony to a lovable Jesus. Cardinal Martini confronts us with Jesus from another viewpoint. Jesus is the friend of tax collectors and sinners. He hears the questions of the young. He brings unrest. He fights with us against injustice.

Night is a time of darkness, imagination, sharpened senses. And "the middle of the night is the beginning of the day." In this sense the conversations in Jerusalem, a place in which Christian history originates, are also conversations about the way of faith in times of uncertainty.

The Cardinal's thoughts and answers, recorded here from our conversations, open the door to a courageous and credible church.

Rev. Georg Sporschill, SJ
Jerusalem, November 2007

1

What Sustains Life?

Dear Father Georg,

It is already late, but the street children have only just gone to sleep. Now it is finally quiet in the Lazarus Social Center. Almost all of us volunteers from Austria and Germany have sat down to gather together our questions for Cardinal Martini. Most of us would gladly go with you to Jerusalem to meet him personally. He must be a great person, with so much courage and so open to our questions. Please don't just ask him about religion, but also about his life. We are very curious. Please forgive me for leaving the questions at your door. It is past midnight.

Yours,
Wenzel

As a Cardinal and theologian, what do you say to someone who doesn't believe in God?

I would have a lot of questions for him. What is important to him? What are his ideals? What are his values? I would need to discover these things. I wouldn't try to convince him of anything, but would say to him instead that he should try living life without a belief in God, and think deeply about himself. Perhaps in some situations he will experience a certain hope, or notice what gives life meaning and joy. I would wish him to have conversations with people who are seekers or believers. Perhaps God may give him the grace to recognize that he does exist.

Why do you yourself believe in God? And how do you experience him?

My parents gave me the gift of belief in God; my mother taught me to pray. At school friends were important for me; they strengthened my belief. My homeland of Italy is a part of Christian Europe. Those who open their eyes to it can see much evidence of faith. As a Jesuit I have been strengthened in my relationship with God by the Spiritual Exercises of St. Ignatius. John, the beloved disciple, is my companion in friendship with Jesus. Many tasks in my life, including the difficulties, have shown me that I can have faith. War, terrorism, personal fears—how often have I been rescued! I have met many good people. Life has shown me that God is good and prepares the way for us all.

My job has always been to speak about faith. Most of my learning has come through that. Often it is enough just to listen well. In the diocese of Milan young people have often helped me to seek answers to new questions. Mostly you learn to have faith when you lead others to faith.

To experience God is both the easiest and the most important thing in life. I can experience him in nature, in the stars, in love, in music and literature, in the words of the Bible, and in many other ways. It is an art of attentiveness, just as you must learn the art of loving or the art of being conscientious in your work.

Are there moments when you argue with God?

In everyday things I have had few difficulties. There was, however, one major question: at first I could not understand why God allowed his Son to suffer on the cross. Even as a bishop, sometimes I could not look up at the cross because this question bothered me. Then I would argue with God. Death makes it clear that all people must die. Why does God want that? By the death of his son he could have spared all people from death. In my struggle I was helped at quite a late stage by a theological thought: without dying we would not be capable of giving ourselves completely to God. For our own security we would look for ways out. That is not self-giving. In death, however, we are forced to put our hope in God and to believe in God. I hope that in death I will be able to say this *yes* to God.

Does a bishop, and a theologian, also have problems that are a burden to his faith?

Burdens are fears, too little trust in God. Whenever God gave me a job I didn't think I would be able to do, perhaps to be a bishop or a professor at a large university, to speak with terrorists, to hold the European Church together, or to answer questions from the Pope; here, I must say, I sometimes had reservations. Also, it was sometimes difficult in conflicts. I didn't argue with God, but I asked him, *Can I do that? Why must I? Am I the right person?*

I have been most ready to argue with God when I faced separations and farewells, when people left me or I had to leave people. Or when I felt powerless. God sometimes gives you big tasks, entrusts many people to you, and you have very few possibilities available to you.

That leaves you hurt. Then I would ask God, as the psalmists do, *Why must this be?* I would then come to see that out of doubt comes something new and more profound. At first it was always difficult, when you still couldn't see the new part that was coming. Naturally you need a lot of trust in God, but that often begins with doubts, with questions.

I haven't had many reasons to argue with God, because he has guided me all my life and actually rather spoiled me. He has given me a smooth path and put many people at my side who have taught and supported me, and who have needed me. So I have felt more and more loved and accepted by God.

Which question would you ask Jesus, if the opportunity arose?

I would ask him whether he loves me even though I am so weak and have made so many mistakes; I know it and yet I would really like to hear it from him again, that he loves me.

I would also ask him whether he will come for me at my death, whether he will receive me. I would ask that in my dark hours of separation or death he might send angels, saints, or friends who will hold my hand and help me to overcome my fear.

Earlier, as a bishop and with responsibility for the Church, I would have asked Jesus, *Why do you allow this gulf between many young people, especially those who lack for nothing, and the Church with every heavenly treasure it can offer to people? Why can't the two sides come closer together?* I would ask him, *Why do you allow many young people to become indifferent, so that they sometimes lose even the joy of life?*

As a bishop I asked God many a time, *Why don't you give us better ideas, why don't you make us stronger in love, more courageous in dealing with current issues?* Or, *Why do we have so few priests? Why are there so few in the orders, although they are sought for and needed?* I asked him those things earlier on. Today I ask, or rather request, that he receive me, and when the going gets difficult, that he not leave me.

We Christians believe that everything is created from love. So where does evil come from? Why is there so much suffering?

When I look at evil in the world, it takes my breath away. I understand people who come to the conclusion there is no God. Only when we view the world—as it really is—with the eye of faith can anything change. Faith awakens love, which in turn brings us to be involved on behalf of other people. From self-giving comes hope in spite of suffering.

Sometimes we see in retrospect that evil brings out good qualities in people. For me, evil consists in those circumstances which give rise to street children, homeless people, and asylum seekers, those who seem to have no place in the world. And "the sins of the world" are the natural catastrophes in which thousands of people are carried off.

But I experience again and again that this evil awakens many good qualities. People wake up and say: I want to help! Evil here brings out the best in people. That is not a satisfactory explanation, but we do know that we can learn a lot from suffering.

No one can answer the question about the origin of evil. But there are hints: God has given people freedom. He does not want robots or slaves, but partners. Partners answer any offers with yes or no, they love or they don't love, they are not compelled to anything.

With freedom, however, come some difficulties as well. You can say "no," even to God's love, even to God. If God says: *I need you, I am calling you,* people can answer: *I don't want to, I prefer something else*—money, instant gratification. In this way some people make others unhappy, and in the end they make themselves unhappy as well. People don't always use their freedom for good. They destroy others, the environment, themselves.

If we were to face the choice: do we want people who can do no evil and are not free, who are robots and slaves, or do we want free people who love, who can say yes and no?—then my answer is, I thank God for freedom, with all the risks that go with it. Love comes from the mystery that God takes us seriously as partners. We must work hard at our response to the love of God.

Why do some people have a good life and others not?

Who has a good life? I know people in poor countries who are wretchedly poor and still much happier than many people in rich Europe. There are poor rich people and rich poor people. In any case, wealth is dangerous; we must be careful to use it for our happiness and for wider justice, so that it doesn't become a burden. Jesus expressed this very real concern with the words: "It is easier for a camel to pass through the eye of a needle than for a rich man to enter the Kingdom of Heaven."

Nevertheless we must not ignore the fact that some people have a bad life, go hungry, and are not spared serious illness.

If we can't answer the question Why, *there is another question:* How *can we live with suffering and misfortune?*

An initial thought: Misfortune is like a thorn and a constant challenge. How do healthy people react to a disaster? When they hear about it, they think, *I must do something about that.* That happened to me when Italy was suffering under terrorism. I knew I had to visit those people in prison. They were really the unlucky ones. I met aggressive, belligerent and despairing people who were to spend their whole lives in prison.

When I meet misfortune and summon up the courage to do something about it, a certain dynamic kicks in, in which the unhappy become happier and the happy more grateful. They become aware of how much they can do. They no longer say, *that's the way things are.*

A second thought: a lot of misfortune is caused by people. That forces us to think politically and to fight for justice, for a place for children, for the old, the ill, to fight against hunger, against AIDS. With the resources and means used to produce weapons and fight wars, we human beings can do a lot of positive things. There are other, better goals for which these same resources can be used.

A third consideration: we should ask ourselves, *How am I involved in this misfortune and responsible for it? For the destruction of the environment, for global warming, for unemployment, for the radicalization of religion and of the oppressed?* We should ask not only, *Why is that, dear God?* We should ask also, *What is my part in this and how can I change the situation?* And further: *What limits and what sacrifices am I prepared to make so that something will change?*

If I am not able to answer completely the question about suffering, I can at least question my own life: *Where can I do something to make things better?* If I ask that question, a lot of misfortune and unhappiness can change. I see that especially in young people. Many of them sit in front of the TV or computer and are swamped with terrible images. So they take refuge in other worlds. A few, however, stand up and go to the suffering people; they help and learn that they can be life-savers. They discover possibilities that can only be brought to reality by active people, and not passive consumers.

A young woman who gives language lessons to asylum seekers and helps them to find their way in a wealthy society said to me: "Poverty as I see it on TV is terrible. Now I am in the midst of it and I suddenly feel a happiness I didn't know before I came here. Suddenly I am aware of how strong I am. I didn't know that earlier. I am discovering that many of these foreigners are wittier, more imaginative, more religious, and better friends than many of the good people I know."

With young drug addicts I have seen that their friends and colleagues have woken up and recognized what can happen because of one apparently small and stupid action. Someone had endangered, or perhaps even destroyed, his life. When their eyes were opened, they didn't do these stupid things any more. There are many sides to this work, which only the good Lord knows in its entirety.

Misfortune has many layers. My trust has become greater and stronger than suffering. My faith in God is hopefully so strong that it will win through in the misfortune of sickness and the loneliness of death. In my life up till now I have experienced a lot of terrible things; war, terrorism, problems in the Church, my own sickness and weakness. And yet, all that becomes part of the many experiences of an eighty-year-old life. My bad times are small in comparison with the good times. The good times are there to be shared. Above all, good fortune is not something that comes to you, something you just wait for. Good fortune must be sought.

Do you have an answer to the question, What does God want from us?

God wants us to trust—to trust him and also to trust one another. Trust comes from the heart. If we have enjoyed many good experiences—as a child, with parents, with other people we like—we will become secure, strong people. People who have learned to trust are not anxious; rather, they have the courage to get involved, to protest when someone says something disparaging, evil, or destructive. Above all, they have the heart to say *yes* when they are needed. God wants us to know that he is on our side. God can make us strong. You can't do some great work, whether it is reaching out to street children or the homeless, or leading a church, and say you are doing it on your own. If you don't trust that you are receiving supernatural or divine strength, then that is simply arrogant. God wants people who count on his help and his power. They can transform the world, especially suffering and injustices, so that the world will be as God created it and wants it to be: full of love, justice, cared for, and interesting. And for that He wants us as co-workers.

What are possible steps on the way to God?

For young people a first step is the question: *What task is being given to me in life? What must and can I do?* Whoever asks these questions becomes a co-worker with God in the world; such people sense that God needs them and supports and accompanies them.

When you are tired, when you don't understand something, perhaps you then learn to pray, or to reach back to what you have learned earlier as a child and perhaps not understood. Much later, in some difficult situation or in the face of a large undertaking, the prayer you have learned earlier, and repeated without thinking much about it, suddenly acquires power.

We need to plan the way to God as we would plan a day's hike or mountain climbing. If you want to climb a mountain you have to go into training beforehand. Just as we can train for physical strength, so we can also train for spiritual strength. If I am always watching TV or constantly sitting in front of the computer, the "muscles" of love, imagination, and the connection to

God become weaker and weaker. I think we need to do exercises; these exercises are prayer, spiritual exercises, conversations, and social engagement. Whoever does these things draws nearer to God. He or she senses more strongly a growing partnership with God.

One step on the way to God could be to become a "missionary," to live one's "mission." What does that mean? Many of us have a wonderful life compared to others. It is worthwhile learning to pass one's good fortune along. But that doesn't happen automatically. Just as a car salesman must learn his job, we need to learn to master our tasks. How can we pass on our faith, our idealism, our trust, and our love to others who are sick or alone or who cannot love?

Steps on the way to God: that can also mean going into a foreign culture, getting to know other religions, or learning a foreign language, so that understanding and peace can grow.

A further step is just to look. If I see what is beautiful, I can't explain it, but the wonder of it can lead me to God. If I then sense that God will not allow me to fall and that he strengthens me, or if I undertake ambitious projects, then he surprises me again and again. In silence, in calmness, and in listening, one comes very close to God.

We are also allowed to fight with God as Jacob did, to doubt and struggle like Job, to grieve like Jesus and his friends Mary and Martha. These are all ways that lead us to God.

In the end, does God lead everyone who yearns for him to himself?

I hope that sooner or later God redeems everyone. I am a great optimist. I do admit that in many people I can't see it happening. There are times also in my own life when I don't feel redeemed. My hope has nevertheless become stronger that God receives all of us, that he is merciful. On the other hand, naturally, I can't imagine how Hitler or a murderer who has abused children can be with God. It's easier for me to think that such people are simply extinguished. That's the way we think in this world. But perhaps in the other world God has new possibilities. That is an open question. That is a question for God.

There is the image of purgatory in which such people—to put it in modern terms—undergo therapy until they can open up and receive the love of God. It is beyond our imagination that someone who has turned away from God like this, who in our estimation is completely evil, can be saved by this generous and merciful God.

But there is the image of the punishing judge, of the justice of God.

Jesus fought in God's name for us to live justly. And "justly" is not simply to treat one another lawfully, but to look out for one another, to protect the weak, and to be helpful. That is what Jesus intended with pictures of the judge and of judgment. The question is: Am I an optimist or a pessimist? Does God still have something else in mind, when we have exhausted all earthly possibilities? Yes, there is hell, but nobody knows if anyone is there. However, we have to reckon with it. There is hell, and in fact hell on earth. There are situations so complicated that one is stuck in a deadlock: being trapped, no way out, being "eternally" lost— that is hell. When I think of addicts, the terminally ill, and what people do to one another, I always think, that is hell. And Stalingrad or the Holocaust, they are both really hell.

Hell in the teaching of Jesus is a warning to us to live so that we never produce this hell and never get into it. The decisive message is that Jesus wants to shield us and free us from these forms of hell. We must watch that we don't fall into one. And we must help others to ensure that they don't either. Hell is a warning, a threat, a reality. But I remain with my belief that, in the end, the love of God is stronger.

And what is the meaning of the concept of purgatory?

Purgatory is one of the human concepts of a way to spare people from hell. The Church developed the idea of purgatory, which claims that even if you are a person who has created so much suffering and produced so much hell, perhaps even after death there is still some place where you can be cured, where you can change your ways and where you have another chance. It is actually the extension of the opportunity to change, and in this respect it is an optimistic idea.

What characterizes a good Christian?

A good Christian is one who believes in God and trusts in him, who knows Christ, is getting to know him better, and listens to him. Getting to know means reading the Bible, talking with Christ, responding to his call, and growing more like him. A Christian is someone who knows his love for Jesus is becoming stronger. All this brings him more and more into social action, being involved with others as Jesus was, as he healed people, called disciples, criticized the powerful, warned the rich, and welcomed strangers. In this way you become a person who feels supported by God. At your death you can hopefully say to God: *You are carrying me, I am hidden in you, you are taking me to yourself.*

Can this goal be reached through education? Or in other words, what should religious education be like?

Religious education is not easy today, because our world with all its offerings is saturated with values that contradict this aim.

One example is Sunday. It's not easy for a priest when everyone on Sunday is heading out of town to the country, or has to work. Or just think of all that's on offer for young people at weekends. In my childhood we went to Church without question and we prayed at mealtimes. We didn't read the Bible so often; Christian families today read the Bible much more, and the Bible and the values of other religions are presented more fully to children.

Many simple customs also belong to a Christian upbringing; we need only think of the festivals: Christmas, Easter, weddings, funerals. We should also be aware of what Christianity gives us by showing us how one can celebrate and recognize the high and low points of life, so that people can be comforted and take heart.

Christian upbringing also requires, of course, the training of one's critical faculty and the expression of one's own opinion. To listen to and take seriously the questions and understandings of youth is one condition of a religious education.

The basis of a Christian education for me, however, is the Bible. When that is the foundation, there are many possibilities and ways to lead everyone to the one God. If we don't think biblically, we become limited and blinkered and do not have God's vision.

Whoever reads the Bible and listens to Jesus will discover how Jesus was amazed at the faith of the Gentiles. It's not the priests that he puts up as models, but the heretics, the Samaritans. When he is hanging on the cross, he accepts the thief into heaven. The best example is Cain: God gives Cain a sign by which he is protected and no one can kill him; but prior to that, Cain was guilty of the murder of his brother.

The whole Bible expresses the theme that God is one who loves the foreigner, who lifts up the weak, who wants us to help and serve all people along our various paths.

Human beings and even the Church, however, are always in danger of seeing themselves as absolute.

How can we face the danger of narrow-mindedness?

We have to work on living out the breadth of "Catholicism," and we must get to know others, for example, Muslims. Many say that Muslims are in favor of a holy war, that they would all more or less want to convert us by force. That may be partly true, but it is not supported by the Qu'ran. People distance themselves from their basic text, from the Ten Commandments, and carve out a new religion for themselves. This danger exists for us too. You can't make God a Catholic. God is beyond all the barriers and borders we create. We need borders in life, of course, but we mustn't confuse them with God, whose heart is always bigger. He is not to be domesticated or tamed. I don't know any better way to ensure this breadth of thinking than to read the Bible. If we do that, we can enthuse others and share with them the treasures we find in the Bible. Anyone who finds a good Bible teacher is indeed lucky.

God leads us outward if we listen to Jesus and notice the poor, the oppressed, and the sick, and if we reach out to these people and touch them. Then God teaches us to think broadly.

What is the position of a Christian in today's world?

A Christian doesn't lose himself in modern trends, in what happens to be fashionable and what everyone wants. The Christian interferes, takes action, and speaks his mind. "You are the judges of the world," says Jesus to his disciples and to us. He thereby puts us into a position of power. We are to help the world find direction; that is the meaning of being a judge. We are not just a drop in society's river, but we are to decide where this society should go. This means that living as a Christian in society is not always easy.

A basic principle of Christianity, actually the Christian principle, is love of God and love of others. Is love "the highest of the emotions?"

Yes, but not everything that at first seems to be, and goes by the name of love, is in fact love. Business, advertising, and even pornography use this word. Everything beautiful and good can also be misused.

Nothing is more precious than love. When I think of friends, of my parents, of young people—of which of them can I say "they like me, I like them, I trust them?" Or is there anything greater than when young people are in love?

What is true love?

There are moments when we know if love is deep and perhaps even perfect. For example, in a conflict or an argument (things that are always happening in life), if a relationship is solid, then a couple or a family can be at loggerheads but not break up because of it; instead they become even more deeply bonded. Then they can say: *Our love is stronger than all our conflicts.* A love that is fearful and avoids conflict is not as strong as this.

If I am rapt and in love today, that is wonderful. But if after forty years my parents are still married and can say, we belong together, we have children together, we have a good life—although they are only too aware of everyday life and all that each of them has to put up with—then they, I believe, have a strong or perfect love.

This is also true of work. I might do one year of social work, or I might want to give my whole life to this work. I become a member of a club or a group, or I commit my life to the Church, to a woman, to a man. Whenever I make that leap into a commitment, there is a strong love. You can't create it, but when it is given to you, I believe it is complete, perfect.

Is love something boundless?

Yes, love is boundless. If you take "boundless" literally, love leads to God. But love is also a very practical matter. Young people need to learn to get along with one another, even in a physical sense. And the social aspect must be learned, and praying too; all these are forms of love, in which experiments are allowed and there is no reason to be afraid. You should always listen deeply within yourself to discern whether something is happening because of love, or because of pure momentary desire. Your own heart and your grounding in the Church will give you the answer to this.

I can have a relationship filled with pleasure, but afterwards I know it was not love. In this case, to be self-critical and also to learn from negative experiences is important. In this way you progress toward the perfection of love. You can't learn that at your desk. And here I see a challenge for the Church: to be a companion to people along the path of love, to ask them questions, to stand beside them, often in silence, so that they can go forward with this discovery, step by step, on the path of love and therefore on the path to God.

What is the difference between God's love for people and love between people?

The love of God is very resilient; it doesn't collapse so quickly. The love of God endures everything, while human love sometimes cracks at the edges. God doesn't seek advantage. The love of God is free from side issues and from any purpose. People sometimes love another only because he or she is young and beautiful, or they only want the youth in the other person. God's love on the other hand is pure and unconditional. It is stronger. And it is gratis. It is not deterred by the weaknesses and mistakes of people. On the contrary, particularly in weakness, just at that very point when you really need it, you feel the love of God most especially. With people it is often the opposite. They regard the weaknesses of the other person as a reason to leave. God would say, you need me especially and I love you especially.

What characterizes Jesus' love?

Through his life and his words, Jesus made the love of God visible. I think especially of the fact that he had many friends. He called his disciples and lived together with them. They were able to observe him at work, preaching and healing. They were able to travel with him. They observed him at prayer. He was a master of friendship and that characterizes his love.

Also characteristic of the love of Jesus is certainly his closeness to the poor. Jesus lived very simply in order to be close to everyone. He chose a homeless life in order to be there for all people, and not to build any wall around himself. Jesus went out to meet the stranger. And most important of all: he was able to pass this love on. His love was on the offensive. He didn't simply stay at home feeling comfortable, but went from village to village, from town to town. He went where there were conflicts, where he needed to bring his love to bear, so that there could be peace between Jews and non-Jews, between Israel and the Romans. He took the risk of entering into such conflicts and showed that God's love must change the world and these conflicts.

For that he risked his life and finally gave up that life on the cross. But even before that we see his self-giving in the deep friendship with his disciples, and in his sensitivity, his empathy with all people who suffered. That is his love, I believe, which I experience in communion, in prayer, with my friends, in my work.

What is the most important rule Jesus taught for living with one another?

The most important is: you should love your neighbor—you will love your neighbor—as yourself. Or, as it is written in the original Hebrew: you will love your neighbor because he is like you. If I know that the next man is carved from the same wood as I am, that he has the same strengths and weaknesses as I have, this closeness also gives me the power to love him. If I feel myself separated from another person, and I think to myself that he is bad and I am good, that he is weak and I am strong, then I don't love him. If I know that we are all in the same boat, this thought awakens in me empathy and love.

You will love your neighbor because he is like you, says Jesus. And he says something even greater: *You will love as I have loved you.* How is that possible? People who are faithful to Jesus understand that.

Jesus quotes Holy Scripture, our Old Testament, when he says we must protect the weak and pardon the guilty. We must learn to resolve conflicts, dissolve enmities, and establish peace.

This active way of loving is the most important rule for living that Jesus gives people. It means also, never stand back, never say, we're fine and have nothing more to contribute.

We should ask ourselves as well: *What am I called to do? What is my task in life? Why has God given me all these gifts? Why is he showing me the world?* Asking questions like this, I call it political thinking. I am one who receives from God directions and especially strength, and a call to do something in the world, so that it will again be the way God originally created it.

If Jesus lived today, what would be his most urgent concern? What would he see as the greatest problem of our time?

I think he would wake up the well-off young people and bring them onto his side, so that they, together with him, could change the world. And changing the world means taking away people's fears, stemming aggression, and removing injustices between rich and poor. And above all, giving people a place to live, so that they feel welcome, whether they be children, foreigners, old people, the sick, or the dying. For this task I think Jesus would seek out the strongest people, and they are obviously the young. As he originally did, Jesus would make apostles of young people. "Apostle" means "one who is sent": active, confident, open people who share their lives with him.

If he wanted to enthuse young people and make disciples out of them as he once did, would he treat the Catholic Church today as he did the Pharisees in his own day?

Yes. Jesus loved the Pharisees. They were his partners, his colleagues. He discussed and argued with them. I think if he returned, he would do that even more. He would be involved in struggles with those in positions of responsibility in the Church and remind them that their work involves the whole world; that they are not here for navel gazing, but need to look out beyond the borders of their own institution. Naturally, to those who declare themselves his followers he would give courage, and this would hurt some people. He would not so much criticize those in authority as show them how much hard work still needs to be done. He would be full of encouragement, because so much happens today out of fear.

There is not only fear, but also indifference. What is Jesus' reaction to that?

In fact both exist in the Church, fear and indifference. Jesus will wake up and shake those who are indifferent, and he will encourage the fearful. And of course he will start with his own people. The goal of all churches, all religions, is to do good in the

world and to make the world a brighter place. And Jesus will
make them better able to carry out that task.

How can one live in the Church today?

Today it is difficult to belong to the Church and simply be a
passive member. But whoever gets involved and takes on some
responsibility can really make a difference. When I was a young
man, and then even later when I was a bishop, working with
young people was what helped me most to be a Christian. We
can say with Paul: I am "another Christ." Today he has no other
hands, no other mouth than yours and mine. If you put yourself at the disposal of Christ, if you know that you are supporting his Church, you will learn to love it, even if the Church
causes you pain.

Today there is a whole spirituality market: Esotericism,
Buddhism, Yoga. How can the Church survive and win over
young people?

Buddhism and Yoga are wonderful ways into a deeper life,
but so are the spiritual exercises of St. Ignatius. What distin-
guishes us from the others is Jesus and his way. A Christian can
only survive among the offerings in the religious and pseudo-
religious marketplace if he knows Jesus. A Christian becomes
familiar with the Bible, acts in the name of Jesus, visits prisoners, tends the sick, and stands up for justice. A Catholic
Christian receives Jesus at Communion.

The Church needs youth and it can develop new spiritual
forms. However, I wouldn't like to give up on the older generation. They are faithful Christians and can teach children by their
example. Faith in God and friendship with Jesus will be passed
on across the generations.

There are many contradictions between preaching and action. How do I recognize faith and truth?

God lights the fire of devotion. If I allow that fire to be lit, it is easy to recognize God. Without my devotion God remains a distant mystery.

For my faith in God, Jesus is my teacher; even more, he is my friend. The most important thing is to hear his voice in the Bible. Everybody can learn to hear that. Conscience speaks to everyone.

Certainly there is a lot of hypocrisy and also weak Christians, and also weak priests who are overburdened. Ideally you should help someone you think is a hypocrite, not by telling him he is a hypocrite, but rather by helping him in his weakness. Offer him your friendship. You can change him.

I find certain types of people unlikeable, but I am supposed to love them. How is that possible?

Love begins with shared actions. When you are with people you don't like, you have to acknowledge your feelings. There is no point in lying to yourself. And you can't directly change those negative feelings. Treat such relationships as a training ground; think about why the other person is unlikeable. Look for the attractive qualities in her that she surely has. Take note as to whether something in you changes because of that. Jesus has shown us that it is possible to learn and practice getting along with one's enemies, and to "de-enemy" them, as the Jewish theologian Pinchas Lapide says.

How should I treat those of other faiths?

First of all, it's a good idea to ask that person what is important to him about his religion. You can also find out a lot about

Islam, Judaism and the Eastern religions through good literature. Get this other person to invite you to a prayer or worship service, and take him some time to a Church service. If you are going to enter another religious world, you need a friend to accompany you there. That won't take you away from Christianity, but will deepen your Christian life. Don't be afraid of what is strange or different.

I have a friend who would like to pray but can't. How would you show this person how to pray?

The only way is my own daily prayer. I pray quite simply. Everything that occurs to me, everything I have to do that troubles me, also whatever brings me happiness, and especially the people I think of, I bring all this before God. I talk with him quite normally, not at all piously. In prayer I feel as if someone is supporting and holding me, even when I can see lots of problems, even the weaknesses in the Church. When I pray I see light. My hope grows stronger as well as my strength to do something. My confidence grows.

If you want to help your friend, then pray. If he wants to pray, then he is already quite close to God. Find a place where you and others can pray with him. It's easiest for people of the same age to show each other how to pray. He will find his way to prayer via the bridge of friendship.

How did you learn to pray?

I was very lucky. In my family and among my friends it was part of life to pray. Prayer and Church were as natural as eating. I'll never forget how we prayed during the war. Somehow I knew: *you are protected, you need have no fear, even when the bombs are falling.* We have a father in heaven who is keeping an eye on us. He helps us even when we make mistakes.

Today there are not so many families who pray. We also have no war in our country—thank God. Is there another way to prayer except by suffering and danger?

Certainly. The question is: Who is inviting you to pray? I think of a congregation that holds a Taizé service to which many young people come. It is at 6 a.m. The priest invites the young people to breakfast afterwards and everyone is happy to come. It is a good opportunity to show young people in their confirmation preparation how others pray. The Sunday morning service is hard to take for many. Prayer groups and discussion groups can lead them to it, especially services that they can prepare themselves. "The Spirit blows where it will"—be surprised by God.

What is the significance of the Mass, or rather attendance at Mass on a Sunday, for young and old?

The Sunday Mass is open to all. It requires consideration of one another, especially the serving of others. It is good if we can think: *What can we contribute so that both the old and the young enjoy this service?* A Mass cannot be self-centered.

The Mass is needed by everyone who wants a living relationship with Jesus and his fellow Christians, because Jesus himself instituted the Last Supper. It is the most important way to meet him. In this celebration we hear the words of the Bible so that we can reflect on life. The Bible is the book that makes people Christian, and in this celebration Jesus joins with us, because he wants to be our friend.

Many say that Christianity gives people a guilty conscience. Is that true? And what is the real meaning of "conscience"?

The German philosopher Herbert Schnädelbach made this criticism in a well-known article on the "seven birth defects of a geriatric world religion." He took the unforgettable *mea culpa* of Pope John Paul II as a basis for writing "The Curse of Christianity."

For my part I can say I was lucky in the development of my conscience. I owe that to good upbringing. My parents and the educators at the Jesuit school were strict, but they didn't instill a guilty conscience in me. They were open-minded and gave me different perspectives. We learned to assume responsibilities in the community and to lead others. We strove toward great goals. This education awakened our ambition and made us strong. We also learned confession. I understand confession as release and liberation, not oppression. The times are long gone when the Church could talk you into having a guilty conscience.

We don't need a guilty conscience, but rather a sensitive conscience: one that lets us feel where our boundaries lie, both personally and in the community. What is important is sensitivity and the courage to assume my responsibilities. Where am I needed? Working for peace is included here too. There are always conflicts. Free of any guilt feelings, a Christian will have ideas on how to dissolve enmities, how to create peace and bring people together.

Someone who died for his conscience was the Austrian Franz Jägerstätter, whom the Church declared a saint in 2007. He was executed by the Nazis in 1943 because of his statement that he could not be a National Socialist and a Christian at the same time: "there are things in which one must obey God rather than men."

I know there are people who suffer because of a guilty conscience. They need divine forgiveness. A spiritual companion or therapy would help them. A guilty conscience can be healed, new strength released, and the joy of life awakened by conversations in a confidential atmosphere. If I have done something bad, or omitted to do something, a guilty conscience is healthy; to have a guilty conscience for no reason is a sign of illness.

On the subject of conscience the Second Vatican Council says: "Man has the law of God written in his heart; to obey that is his dignity and according to it he will be judged. Conscience is the innermost core and shrine of man, in which he is alone with God." (*Church and World* 16) It is our job to give people courage and joy, not only with words but also with grand visions. Then young people will understand that it is worth getting involved. And, being able to share in God's aims, we are enabled to bring our own offerings. Our conscience opens us up to divine visions, and so our lives grow in confidence.

Nevertheless, the Church talks a lot about sin. Does it really want to make people worse than they are?

The Church has talked a lot about sin, too much. It can learn from Jesus that it is better to give people heart and to challenge them to fight against sin in the world. The Bible's intended meaning of the sin of the world is not only our personal failings, but all the injustices and burdens that we inherit. Jesus calls us to cooperate in healing, wherever the divine order of the world is damaged.

The Church is against sex before marriage. But who obeys that any more? Nobody can do that.

In answering this question, I would like to begin by talking not about sex, but about erotica. To be forbidden any love that also has expression in physical tenderness would be inhuman. Adopting rules to prepare oneself for a man/woman commitment is important, just as learning to love with body and soul. However, if you don't keep something for that time of commitment and marriage, if you take everything beforehand, then there is a very great danger that you will fail in your relationship through human weakness and ignoring boundaries. The love between two people is always unique. So it is advisable to protect yourself against a "closing down sale."

If a man (or woman) has already experienced everything physically possible with many other women (or men) before or outside marriage, there is almost no room for the discovery of new experiences between them. That is too little for a marriage, which is not a matter of luck and chance.

Having no sex is unnatural. So why are priests not allowed to marry?

In all churches except the Roman Catholic Church priests can marry, even in the Greek Catholic. The idea of priests not marrying came from the monastic life. Men and women live together in communities or as hermits in order to follow Jesus in his celibacy. They want to be completely free for God's service. "To love God with all one's heart, mind and strength," as it says in the Hebrews' creed, is for some people really everything. They give their lives out of love for *God*.

For celibacy it is important that the community gives the priest a place of love and security. A priest should not feel alone, even though his most important times are those of prayer. We shouldn't forget that the Roman Catholic Church didn't legislate for the celibacy of priests until the Tridentine Council in the sixteenth century, even though compulsory celibacy had existed since the eleventh century.

The Church as an institution often seems very weak. Who is to blame for that?

Some think that the old men of the Church wouldn't have anything worthwhile to say to our times. On the other hand, young people are not saying anything; they are not taking part in the Church. Now whether the young are not saying anything or the old are not listening to anything, the question of blame takes us nowhere. Communication between the generations must be improved, because they really have a lot to say to each other. They don't need to agree, but rather to challenge each other and bring one another further along the path to God. That is precisely why a conversation is needed.

The greatest suffering of the Church in affluent countries, in the West, is certainly that this communication has become weak. Dialog is important, and in my opinion also argument, between young and old, between tradition and modern questioning. I would be very happy if this dialog again became a dynamic force. Then we could teach one another to love and we would be more capable of loving. We would feel so secure in God that we could dare to engage with all issues, problems, and conflicts.

Why are you Roman Catholic? Couldn't one change one's Church if it's antiquated?

I'm a Catholic, my parents were Catholic and they introduced me into the Church. It could have been different, just as with the relationships that are given to us. It's chance or fate. When you are brought into a denomination, there are tests that follow. Whether you are young or grown up, you must decide what you really want. Some people change their affiliation or, sadly, they do nothing at all about it. During my long life I have been in touch with many different churches and religious communities. In many communities that were foreign to me I have found acquaintances and friends, even in Judaism and Islam. And yet that has never made me think of no longer wanting to be Catholic. On the contrary, the more I live with other people, the more I love the Church. I can only recommend seeking contact with believers in other faiths. They will ask you, *Why are you Catholic?* A Muslim will ask you, *Why are you a Christian?* Then you will look for an answer and bear witness to your faith. You will be glad you are Catholic, and you will even be glad that the other person is Protestant or Muslim. These different families are there so that as many people as possible can be helped, and so that they will find a home in God. Religious communities serve to build up and strengthen people and to lead them to God.

As in every relationship, our church life has its highs and lows. We are on a path with the Church. Catholic means all-embracing. That is an invitation to everyone. Evangelical means to live by the Gospel. We are all invited to do that too. Orthodox means "right-believing." We are Orthodox, Evangelical, and Catholic—every Christian can claim that. And yet each one of us belongs to a particular family that is distinct from another.

Loyalty to the family is important. We must not run away from it when things get difficult. That's when it gets really interesting and each individual is important. An aging Church urgently needs young people who will make it strong. The human and sympathetic Church needs you and me perhaps more than a grandiose or powerful Church. Our Church has weaknesses, but by knowing this we stay together and strengthen each other.

What are the most important questions a person should ask him- or herself?

How can I find my own right path? What is my life's task? How can I learn to love myself and others? How do I get the strength, in situations of conflict—in the world as it really is—not to sink, but to be stronger, to be able to change things through the power of hope? How do I go forward each day, in faith, in hope, and in love?

What sort of love do I have and can give? Your career and everything else depends on this.

Young people ask particularly about the meaning of life. What is its meaning for you?

I often hear from young people, "I would like to be happy and loved and I would like to know why I am here." But I would go further: for this happiness it is worth doing some work on finding my right relationship with myself. I have to be careful to stay healthy in order to achieve anything, and also to know my limits and not do too much. Taking care of myself includes sport and prayer. Sometimes pausing and thanking God. Whatever happiness we have already had should not be forgotten in dark times. Whoever is thankful is able to see happiness; such a person feels stronger. Many people are rich and are not aware of it, so they are unhappy.

As well as gratitude, friendship is a source of the meaning of life. Friendship with people I can always question, with whom I can talk not only about my successes, but also about my problems and worries. Friends are those I can confide in when I have lost my strength.

For the meaning of life there are also the people I am there for, and the things I have to do in life. What would I be without the Church? Without conversations with the many people who seek my advice? Without challenges from young people? I have reflected very little on the meaning of life, because I have been allowed to be there for so many people. I say quite consciously "allowed." "Meaning" is like water I swim in.

Meaning evolves. If you make yourself strong for people who come to you needing special protection, and if you become for them advocate, shepherd, and friend, then meaning is intensified in your life and theirs.

Regarding the meaning of life, it is critical for young people that they find the right career and corresponding work, and of course also the right wife or husband. Perhaps also the courage to enter a religious order, and therefore to remain unmarried. The relationship with Jesus, something that can develop in everyone, is for me the deepest source of meaning and the joy of life.

When we face death, the question about the meaning of life becomes absolutely real. Are you afraid of death? What antidote do you recommend for fear?

I am over eighty and you can deduce a fair amount from that. We know how many years a human being is given. The Bible says, when it is mentioned (in Psalm 90), that it is eighty. By this reckoning there is cause for some concern. So there is planning in work and in relationships, to do everything in such a way that it continues on into the future. Whatever I begin, others will have to carry on.

I have concerns when I see how old people get sick, are in pain, and become dependent on others. There is an Indian story in which life is lived in four phases. First of all we learn, then we teach, then we retire and learn to be silent, and in the fourth phase we learn to beg.

I am counting on the fact that God will not demand too much of me; he knows what we can bear. Perhaps when I am dying, someone will hold my hand. I really hope that I will be able to pray at that time. We learn to pray by practicing. Then I will feel that I am being lifted up to God. Death cannot take away this security.

We can strengthen ourselves for the other world, the one we are moving toward, by not living for ourselves but for others, by being aware of the community of the saints. My parents died long ago, but I never forget them. I am grateful to them. I can talk with them. It is a lovely custom to light a candle for those who have died. As you grow older, you have more and more friends in the other world, more than in this world. In the Mass we are in the midst of the community of saints. Our loved ones who are with God gather around Jesus, just like the people with whom we live and work, and especially the people to whom we are grateful. We have a spiritual family, and perhaps street children understand and value that more than we who have been allowed to grow up in security. Benefactors give these children not only money but also, through their involvement and prayers, security.

There is the story of a Protestant theologian who said to his wife on his deathbed, "All my life I have thought about God and the life beyond, and now I do not know anything anymore. Except that I am safe, even in death."

That is also my hope.

2

Courage to Decide

Faith doesn't mean a thing to me. I have nothing against it, but what use is the Church to me? Sure, there is something higher than us. I enjoy nature, I love animals. Friends are the most important things for me, and I would do anything for them. Life is good. What more do I need?

David

The word "more" or magis *is a key word for Jesuits. How would you explain it to David?*

David has everything he needs. Life is good for him. Does he know that for many people life is not good? Other people often have no friends. Others can't believe, as he does, in something higher; they have no optimism. Among young people I often experience sadness, even when they lack nothing.

David doesn't know how lucky he is. He takes for granted his good friends, the beauty of nature, and his many talents. Through his family he has probably been introduced to the Church and faith, those things which no longer have any meaning for him today. Would he perhaps be happier if he could give thanks for these things? Then he will see how much he can do with his talents. He can change the world.

Gratitude leads to *magis*. The person aware of his good fortune wants more. He becomes dissatisfied with the world and acquires an eye for its needs, for what he can do. The key word *magis* describes the dynamism one can experience by giving one's life for others. This is not a life-destroying doctrine. You achieve a richer, more exciting life if you find your task, the task God has intended for you. "More" is the movement toward that something higher.

To look at the world and its needs, to look at oneself and one's gifts, and then to look up—is that the way to see things?

In mountain climbing I look at the peak. I must know my goal. Ignatius Loyola, the founding father of our order, describes the goal of our lives with the famous words: "Man is created to praise God, to show reverence and to serve him." If I look up to God in this way and draw near to him, I get another view of the world. I see what God has given me; I look at the beautiful and the good. And so I am able to give thanks and praise. I open up my inner capabilities. I become an optimist, because I am counting on God's power.

Praising God is the first step. I revere Him by seeking Him, feeling secure in Him, and learning to pray. Learning to pray is the second step. The third step is service. We are co-workers with God, as Paul says. God needs us. Whoever looks at the world, at him- or herself, and up to God will ask him- or herself quite personally: *Lord, what do you want me to do? With these gifts and interests of mine, where can I get involved? Into what problem area do you want to send me?*

The view of the mountain peak awakens a longing in the mountain climber. How does he find the way? In the end, there are many possibilities.

Once you are on your way and wanting "more," you will in fact see many possibilities in front of you. You will recognize many things to be done and you will have to make decisions. Which career will you choose? Do you have the right friends? Who is the right partner for you? Can you imagine for yourself a life in a religious order? It is important to entertain all possibilities and to ask what effect they have on you. Imagine a career as a teacher or engineer. How does the one or other affect your mood? Do you feel nervous or confident, uneasy or relaxed? Are you fearful or do you feel secure? What you experience is called by Ignatius discernment of the spirits. Positive and negative, good and evil spirits influence you. Contradictions, inner conflict, being torn this way and that, wanting "both at once"—these things are the results of these different movements. You can learn to discern the spirits and so acquire important indicators for reaching a good decision.

*St. Ignatius gives us "Rules for the discernment of spirits."
What are they?*

Ignatius names three ways of making a decision. The first is
reason; that is the basis. You can weigh up reasons for a decision.
What speaks for it, what speaks against? It is possible to be completely rational here and to make a list of advantages and disad-
vantages.

In the second way, we pay attention to our feelings. One
imagined situation or another arouses definite feelings, dark or
light, heavy or bright. You might see a dream coming true.
Whenever the possible decision is completely surrounded by a
rosy light, you must be careful. Ignatius speaks of the "bad spirit"
that misleads and deceives. If you achieve peace through this
imagined situation, however, it is very probably a good decision
determined by the good spirit.

As well as reason and feelings, there is sometimes a third
possibility, intuition. Suddenly something becomes clear to you.
You know immediately and with certainty what is right for you.
One example: you interrupt your studies and will be spending a
year doing social work. In this case you must look carefully at
how this fits in with your life in the longer term. Does the decision fit in and is it a continuation of your ongoing social engagement? Or is it completely new, something that contradicts all you
have done before? In the second case you must be careful.
Ignatius would say the "evil spirit" could be at work again here.

Not everything that seems good on first appearance proves to
be so in the long run. Evil wears masks, disguises itself, and comes
under the appearance of Good; these are the temptations we can
be drawn into. Discernment of spirits can be learned. It helps in
the service of God and in making more out of your own life.

To open yourself to the spirits and to allow the new to come to you takes courage. You wish that courage for young people. But is it to be found in the Church?

When I was a bishop, courage was often required of me, although I am rather a more cautious and apprehensive person: meeting terrorists of the Red Brigades, being close to young people, in conversation with priests and co-workers, in the Congregation of Faith, where I spoke completely freely with Cardinal Ratzinger over a ten-year period. And also in the preparation for the most recent papal election, we Cardinals discussed openly among ourselves the questions the new Pope would face and to which he would have to give new answers. Among them, I said, were questions dealing with sexuality and communion for those who are separated and remarried.

Because I am by nature timid, I tell myself when in doubt: Have courage! Abraham was a courageous person. He hardly knew God before God called him. He set off into the distance and left his country, his friends, and his home. God sent him into the unknown and Abraham went. He had the courage to decide. So he became a blessing for many. Still today, the Synagogue, the Church, and the Islamic community live due to his fearlessness. Abraham is the father of all people who believe and have faith. We go into the future with young people leading the way, looking for new paths for humankind. With Abraham I say to my friends just this one thing: Have courage! I wish more of it for us all in the Church.

Why does the Church need this courage?

The situation of the Church in Europe, especially in Western Europe, demands decisions today. There are parishes in which there are no longer any young people. Especially in the large cities, Sunday Church services are held where scarcely a child or young person is present. The coming generation is missing. We could give many reasons for that, often quite practical ones. Young families have moved out of a neighborhood and there are more offices; or foreigners of other faiths have moved in. They often have more children than Catholic families.

I am glad there are many fully alive Catholic parishes, including ones with many young people and very good youth outreach. In spite of that we can't overlook the fact that the Church has lost many young people in these last decades. I ask myself how we can win them back. Where do young people find those treasures without which I can't imagine my own youth? Where are they learning to pray, to seek adventures with others, to get involved in social action? Where do they celebrate festivals? Where do young people get their leadership training? Where do they learn to be good friends, people with an eye for the needs of others? Where then [do they get] the courage to speak to those who are sad or lonely? Where do they learn that self-assurance to be able to offer to help them? Where do they get to know God? Where do they find opportunities to learn about their own religion, about the Bible, the Church, our world and its problems, and also about other religions, with which we compete in many things? A healthy competition, because we are challenging one another.

What do people lack in today's affluent society?
What are the dangers for young people?

Some are perhaps on the wrong track. They will be aware of it. I don't worry about anyone, so long as he or she is on the way. But what about the others? The ones who are trapped in affluence, who are dependent on computers? What about those who are bored? Many turn to drugs or sit alone in front of the television. There are young people who have never been invited to join a community or to work on some large undertaking. They could get the impression that they are not wanted, and that they are not important in making things happen. So when they learn in the papers or on television about world catastrophes, they become depressed, because they have no spiritual strength; they have developed no muscles. By "muscles" I mean that self-confidence that says that I can help and save a life, that I can make people happy, that in fact, things depend on me. Some time or another every young person ends up in need, or faces a life-task that demands of him great strength. Will he have that strength when needed? Where can we find today the training and preparation for the battle against what the Bible calls sin? That doesn't mean primarily our personal weaknesses, but the great injustices and needs of the world against which we are to fight. Jesus wants to free humanity from this distress, which is called sin, because it is not in the divine will. For this reason he committed himself and gave his life to it. And today he is looking for co-workers, especially among young people.

Why does the Church particularly need young people?

Where does a company or a political party look for new workers? First of all among young people, of course. They can be trained and prepared for new tasks. They have energy potential that can still be activated. Among them you will find the highest idealism, and also crazy ideas. Probably the things of the future, the things we are waiting for and need, will find their way into the world most readily via the uninhibited qualities of young people. Even the Church in "old Europe" needs new ideas and a fresh wind. Doesn't youth also need the new, the *magis*, something more than affluence? In the search for the new, I have always seen something positive, the will to change things; and therein lies faith in the Church and our faith in young people. Otherwise it would not be worth criticizing the Church.

Many people tell me that young people used to be more aggressive and critical than they are today. If it has become more peaceful in the world of youth, then I am more disturbed by the thought that they are somewhere else in their hearts, that they are just not interested in the Church and its further development any more, or in the important things to be done in the world. If it gets too peaceful in the Church, if a feeling of satisfaction takes root in society, I think of Jesus' desire to throw a flaming torch of inspiration onto the Earth.

If only it were already burning!

I lived through the Second World War and its aftermath. The poverty and suffering we experienced required all our strength for the reconstruction, for reconciliation, and also for dealing with the guilt. This catastrophe opened up impressive forces all over Europe, in the economy, in politics, and also in the Church. They were stormy times, and they led to the Second Vatican Council and the opening of the Church for the world. I am hoping for a new beginning in the Church, without the need for a catastrophe to wake people up.

What are the great challenges?

The alternative is to recognize the tasks that lie before us. We mustn't play down the crises that already exist; we mustn't look the other way. The great task that confronts us today is the "clash of civilizations" (Samuel P. Huntington); the so-called battle of the cultures. Cultures are colliding with each other, even within Europe. How is Christianity to meet with Islam? Often we don't know what is to be done. I find this helplessness, not knowing what to do, a great burden since I have been living in Jerusalem. Beforehand I was more optimistic, perhaps naïve. Do we know the rules according to which Muslims think and negotiate? Here we find differences between us. Firstly we will want to get to know each other better, in order to understand each other and develop our profile. A crisis is developing here that will confront our children. A child or young person today can no longer, or at least much less than before, live life on a homogeneous social or Church level. It's no longer possible. So in the future there will be a need for more power and ability in making decisions. That is a completely new challenge.

By taking on these challenges, catastrophes can be avoided. There is plenty to do, especially one large undertaking: meeting the needs of the young.

The Church needs young people. Nobody can win over youth better than youth itself; a young person will listen more readily to what is said by another young person. That is particularly the case in personal matters, those concerning friendships, relationships with parents, adventures and secrets—and also God. Young people have the key to the religious area. Earlier it was with the parents, but now it is with youth. The parish, religious education, and the wider Church can only support and encourage the owners of the key. In any case, we can do almost nothing without the possessors of the key.

Nothing gives a priest or a bishop more pleasure than when young people ask questions of him. Good and deep questions presuppose great trust. Trust is the opposite of fear. In meetings with young people I never left them in any doubt that they would have something to say to me, that I wanted to learn from them. Among young people I found friends who later became my greatest helpers in the difficult office of bishop of a large diocese. They told me about their lives, they became part of my own life, and they opened the door to young people for me. Today, I would do even more than I did then; I would invite foreign and especially Muslim young people to meet with me and I would seek their company. Among them are many good people, idealists who would like to work for peace. When they are young, Christians and Muslims can more easily learn to live together, to share matters of faith and together, to be of service to other people.

How did you personally win the trust of young people?

I don't know. It may have begun by chance. As a Jesuit I always lived with young people. As a professor I was dealing with students. I must say that I have always been attracted to difficult people and critical students. Meetings with them always led to the most fruitful discussions. Perhaps in the beginning it was just curiosity. To anyone who wants to be a chaplain today and preach to young people, I can only recommend that he go to young people and look for a teacher among them. My first sermons for youth were given in a very small group, sometimes even to a single person, and then I would ask them to tell me what they thought. I learned a lot; it was particularly in these personal meetings, in which I was the learner, the one seeking help, in which a bridge was built between myself and young people. (At just thirty I was already one of the adults, if not one of the old people.) This bridge is the trust that strengthens every preacher, youth worker, or teacher. When I am met with trust, ideas come and I find the right words. But above all, with my partners in dialog, the young people, I am able to discover and take up new ideas.

So instead of preaching, you allow yourself to be taught by the young. Is this a new pastoral principle?

With young people I have found this pastoral principle, if that's what it is, most strongly confirmed. Nobody in the Church is our object, a case, or a patient whom we need to treat, and certainly not the young. So there's no point in sitting at your desk and thinking about ways to win over young people or how we can build trust with them; that is something they must grant to us. They are the subjects whom we meet, and with whom we seek partnership and exchange. Young people have something to say to us. They belong to the Church, whether or not they agree with our thinking and our opinions, or with regulations. Conversations at eye-level, not looking down from above or up from below, this is what guarantees dynamism for the Church. Then the struggle for answers to questions about modern man will take place in the very heart of the Church.

It is often lamented that young people are only interested in pleasures and diversions, or that when they do get involved in something, it is only in things outside the Church or only for a short time. What would you say to such a diagnosis?

I know there have always been these tendencies, in every generation. My experience of youth is much more positive. We have to distinguish between different groups of young people. Firstly, there are those who have no particular interest in spiritual values, religion, or social issues. They simply live their lives and enjoy themselves, and are concerned with consumption, success, and fun. The Church has almost no contact with them; at best it is superficial and occurs perhaps on the occasion of weddings or funerals.

It's another matter when these young people get into difficulties, when perhaps they become drug addicts or are led into crime. Then they sometimes become aware that they are not on the right path, that they need something else, and depend on others. Then a door might open and the Church can help in a human, social, or therapeutic way. One could say generally that faith must satisfy the whole person, that is, head, heart, hands and feet. Naturally the most important parts happen in the head and heart, but many young people find it easier to start with the hands and feet, especially those who have little contact with the Church or a parish. Courageous involvement for one's brothers and sisters, dedication to one's neighbors, these constitute the right path. (See Matthew 7:11, Mark 12:28-34; Luke 10:25-37.) These people are on the way to the love of God. The Church is there for everyone; it must make no distinction between people who are in and outside the institution.

In this way something might begin to develop, leading the young people further, to faith, trust, or gratitude. Perhaps even into the Church and to Jesus, but we must not make that a requirement. Our help must have no hidden agendas.

A second group are those who come to us because they hope to find among us something they cannot find elsewhere. They come because they need a community and would like to meet other young people. They don't want to be alone, yet questions about prayer or God are less important. Nevertheless, they come closer to us.

As a third group there are many young people who stand for certain values, who are interested in spiritual or social questions, but stay away from the Church. Perhaps they have the same goals—justice, brotherhood of man, solidarity—but they stand for these ideals outside the Church. They are often on the political left. They are working to save the world and for the things that God wants for the world, just as we are. Naturally we would gladly offer them support and also try to work with them. Together we could do a lot more and save more people. Even these young people are often on their own, needing a framework, sharing, a community. We should be showing them where to find sources of strength, recovery, direction; sources of power to help them to find their way through uncertainty and doubt, helplessness and loss of courage.

As a fourth group there are still those young people who come to us and ask: How can I become a good Christian? How can I learn to pray? How can I read the Holy Scriptures? They ask about God and also about their role in the world. Sometimes, however, they have great difficulty opening themselves to God. They find it difficult to pray, they can't decide, can't commit themselves. They are looking for a way to do the will of God, but they are unsure. So they get involved perhaps in good works, but they lack the courage to make a life decision. We must help them to overcome their lack of confidence and indecision, help them to make a decision, even if there is a danger that they will fail.

Young people are on the move—and that is the most important thing.

I hear from young people again and again: "I would really like to be independent."

Independence is a high and important goal. I would say to young people: You must be true to yourself and become strong, through training and hobbies, through the development of your abilities. Whoever loves himself can love other people. Whoever understands herself can also understand others. Faith, trust, and open communication are things to be learned. Hopefully there will be role models and teachers in the Church who can give strength to young people.

God wants us to be independent of all creatures and free of all earthly things to which we cling too closely. Each individual lives in personal partnership with God himself. Nevertheless, independence could be a sign of the fear of attachment, which does present a problem in times of affluence. The flood of input from the media, the computer world, and all the possibilities of consumerism weaken a person's power to make decisions and the capacity for attachment. All these offers and influences, from which there is no escape, demand personalities that can deal with them and use them. An active life, sport and meditation, the formation and care of friendships are important, and certainly also a kind of asceticism, the ability to restrict oneself. Where is the family that places less value on television and the computer and more on eating together, conversation, guests, prayer, going for walks, and taking part in social services? Media outpourings today demand more than ever attention to personal development. How can we teach our young people to listen to their heart and not let themselves be led astray? To belong and to be there for others leads to psychological strength and health.

When you were Archbishop of Milan, you held Bible workshops in the cathedral, and thousands of young people attended. How did you manage to enthuse so many?

In Milan Cathedral we simply tried to listen to texts from the scriptures. A section would be read and then we would remain in silence. That was important so that everyone could find his or her own answer. I didn't give any prepared answers, but only encouragement to listen to the word, attentively and thoughtfully. Nor did I explain very much or give many exegetical comments, but merely tried to confront the young people directly with the text. And so they became familiar with Jesus. They understood that God was asking things of them. Several participants wrote to me years later saying that this communal listening had helped them to come to a decision. They learned to pray with the scriptures and arrived at a point where they recognized: This word is meant for me, quite personally for me, and it has something to say to me.

I think the experience of community was also important. After one of these Bible workshops in Milan Cathedral, where month after month up to five thousand people came to read the Bible with me, I asked once, "Who among you is prepared to follow completely the will of God? Who is interested enough to be totally committed? And many responded, perhaps a hundred. I met regularly with these people after that and worked further with them. I accompanied them on their journey, so that they would get to know themselves and each other better, and be able to discern what they wanted, where their desires were taking them, what their gifts were, where their place in the world was, where they should and could be participating in the work. It is so wonderful to have discovered among so many people those groups and also those individuals who wanted more in the way of dedication, involvement and friendship.

How does one begin such a path with young people?

A great openness is important. It is also important not to be afraid. Why should a person who has set his trust in God be afraid? If I can name only one young person as my friend, I have won the trust of all young people. Then there is that bridge I spoke of, and then the pain and the questions are happening not outside the Church but within it, and even in my own heart. The art of "How do I make friends?" can certainly be learned and improved. There are many books and tips on the topic, which should be studied and put into practice, not only by business representatives but also by agents of the Church.

I know of many initiatives by young people in Italy, going into places wherever there are other young people: in discos, on the beach, on the street. They talk to their contemporaries and get a feeling for their inner needs, even when these are not immediately obvious. They learn to hold conversations and build relationships. Through this they have found that many young people apparently only interested in fun and enjoyment are actually depressed and want to change something in their lives. They say: *I don't know what to do; I need drugs, need alcohol to get by; I am on my own.*

The surprising thing is that increasing numbers of young

people get enthusiastic about the task of approaching others and being aware of where others are in need. It is a wonderful experience for them when they see how easily they are able to find trust, how grateful others are when someone listens to them. It's a job for Church workers to make such relationships possible. Think of the simple principle of the Boy Scouts: do one good deed every day.

3

Making Friends

My best friend has gone to Romania. I don't understand that, because at school she was completely different, totally ambitious. She has often emailed me, and I just can't understand any longer what's going on. She even goes to chapel every day. She is staying for a whole year with her children. I'll have to visit her.

Eva

Without friendship there can be no youth-work. So, can a bishop actually be a friend?

I used to long for friends, but I didn't find any. I wanted too much. I wanted to make friends and was too demanding. These were two mistakes. I could not understand that friends are a gift. I was a bit pessimistic. Later I found a few friends, not many. I am happy to have friends, but I am also happy to be alone. Not until I became a bishop did I experience how good and well-meaning people are. Many priests had a genuine love of their bishop. In this closeness I felt the goodness of God, which I had not earned. Previously I used to spend a lot of time sitting with my books and was shy of being with people. As a bishop, I was overwhelmed by the confidence people placed in me. Young people would approach me, and they dispelled any mistrust.

Friendship for me is something precious and rare; it is given to us by God. I make a distinction between friend and friendly. We should be friendly to everyone, but we cannot be friends with everybody. One sign of friendship is that, when you see someone again after a year, you can talk to him or her as if you had seen each other yesterday. Friends don't have to be together all the time, but can nevertheless always talk together about important things.

How did you find your personal friends?

Ever since I was young, I have loved the mountains. Even when I was Archbishop, I would use my few free hours to be in the mountains, at least half a day a week. My oldest friends are associated with the mountains. We have challenged one another, we have survived dangers, things we never forget. We have shared meals as well as schnapps at the peak. We could walk comfortably in silence. We also talked about personal matters with a frankness almost only possible on a mountain. Think of the experience the disciples had with Jesus on the Mount of the Transfiguration, where they wanted to stay and build huts, where heaven opened to them. Afterwards you have to go down again, to work and struggle to get on with life, but with new energy and knowing about friendship.

Is it really difficult to find friends? Even in unusual situations it is possible to draw near to people. Once when I was much younger, I sat down on a park bench next to a young person who looked to be in a bad way. After some time the lad came to, and looked at me, startled. "Who are you?" The question caught me unprepared. "I'm a priest. Can I do anything for you?" We went together to a little stand-up café, because he was hungry. And so began a relationship in which the world of drugs and therapy was opened to me for the first time. I was actually able to get the young man into a house run by Sisters.

Friendship is something great, but it begins with small things. When I was an educator at a school, I offered coaching in Latin after school (I have always loved languages) and was able to help weak students. I made friends because I was able to be there for these youngsters with their problems at school. They have probably forgotten the Latin since then, but not the friendship. They were especially important to me at that time, because the trust that these schoolboys brought to me spread through the whole class. Perhaps you just have to start with the needs and questions of the young and not with what should be taught to them.

I have not yet mentioned the most powerful means of making friends; in my youth work it was always particularly important. The magic "word" is: make others your helpers. Because I always had a lot to do, and because my studies didn't leave me much spare time, I needed support. During all these periods of overwork, the youngsters helped me most. I would ask one or another to take care of a group session. At the beginning they hesitated; "I can't do that," they would say, or "I'm too young." I would assure them of whatever help they needed and would prepare the session with them. Later I did the same thing with whole groups of leaders. They also needed space where they could report on their successes and ask their questions, and they needed conversations so that they could deal with their failures.

Through companionship with the group leaders I made important friends, of whom several went on to the Ignatian Exercises. They continued to grow. When someone learns from his experiences, grows from that, and is happy, and when another person has been able to contribute to this inner growth, then he will probably be regarded as a friend. A friend enlarges the other person. He discovers his talents and helps him to apply and develop them.

What can we teach young people?

We can't teach young people anything. We can only help them to listen to their inner master. That word is used by St. Augustine, and it sounds strange. It means specifically that we can only create the conditions under which a young person can gain understanding. Understanding and insight must be given to him or her from within.

What do young people need from the Church?
What can they expect?

Young people are interested to learn when they see that, as a result, they will be able to take more responsibility and be taken seriously. The testimony of faith is a simple thing, but it must be practiced. Above all it is important that young people have the courage for it.

Even today I ask friends, preferably younger friends, for ideas and requests before I give a sermon or a lecture. I have frequently done that before speaking with the cardinals. We really want to make the concerns of people and youth our own concerns, and to seek the Church's answers to them. Of course, my young friends are no longer so young; I am all the more interested in conversations with today's youth, be they fifteen, twenty, or twenty-five years old.

It is vital that we first awaken their self-confidence, take note of their talents, offer them our trust, and make friends with them. Then they will come with their questions from life, and out of these will be woven our material to be taught. That is the deepest source from which interest flows.

It is a question of bearing witness. Jesus did not teach his disciples anything else. How did he do that? He let them be part of his life and his work. They had the privilege of asking him questions in his times of retreat and rest. He taught them to make them apostles, able to be sent into the whole world. He taught them to see needs and to attach themselves to those who needed help. This particular attachment makes one inventive. If I love someone who is suffering or being treated unjustly, I become inventive. I have to help him. The spirit opens itself to this imperative, the spirit of advice, strength, and consolation.

When young people take on tasks, they need help and support. There are a lot of basics to be learned, as in most occupations. For example, it is important to learn how to get up in front of a group or in a large space. That includes the right placement of the chair, a microphone test, and the tip for your first appearances to seat your friends in the front rows, friends who send out messages of trust and give you strength. Training in speaking is important; you have to know the rules of group dynamics; and of course, not to forget the right preparation. What is the message I want to get across? What is my aim? What will I achieve? Which points do I want to include? Arranging material in a clear order and in sequence helps. How will I begin the talk? The rhetorical figure *captatio benevolentiae* is a separate art. How will I gain the attention and goodwill of the audience? These are practical things that we learned in our training and are still of use today.

But there is something else: How can I arrange and prioritize my material, so that I don't end up in chaos and miss the vital bits? How can I get organized? How can I get others to share the task with me? How will I deal with them? How will I find the right tone? How can I renew my enthusiasm, when I am despondent and overtaxed?

If someone has decided to become a group leader, he should seek out a master from whom he can learn all of this, and who will be able to continue to help him in difficulties, and who will be a companion to him, especially in relationships, in his personal development, and in everything a leader will experience in the way of beauty and pain. These are the personal abilities and external conditions that make for good learning.

How could the Church open the gates for youth?

We can only open ourselves to youth if we start with youth itself. What are they interested in? Where do they live? How do they live out their relationships? What are they critical of, and what action do they demand of us? There are many issues here in which Church workers can take an active part. To begin with, young people must be central, and only then can adults and Church structures enter the picture, supporting and making adjustments. There is no future in first prescribing for youth how they should live, and then judging them with the intention of winning over those who conform to our rules and views. Communication must begin with complete freedom, otherwise it is not communication. Without freedom nobody can be won over; at best they will be suppressed. The person I meet is a subject from the beginning. In conversation we arrive at new ideas and step forward together.

The young are most sensitive about whether we take them seriously as equal partners, or whether we want to instruct them because they are stupid or mistaken. We believe that all people are creatures of God and of equal worth. That is the critical assumption in every communication we take part in.

But aren't there generational differences? What is the particular contribution of young people?

Of course there are different life situations and stages of life, which modern developmental psychology describes. The Bible, the New Testament, and before that even the Old Testament were also aware of the different stages of life. In his Pentecost sermon, Peter takes a word from the Prophet Joel, who lived in the fourth century before Christ and shows the working of the Holy Spirit in three stages of life, each in a different way:

> "Your sons and daughters will prophesy, your young men will see visions and your old men will dream dreams."

The young people will be prophets; that means they must be critical. The younger generation would not fulfill its task without challenging and criticizing government, leaders, and teachers with its impartiality and unyielding idealism. By being critical, youth carries us, and especially the Church, forward.

The Prophet says that the middle generation, the leaders, will see visions. A bishop, a priest, a father or mother, a businessman—they should set goals for a community, a family, or a company. Those responsible need to know how things will work out and what tasks they have to assume.

It is so nice that the Prophet also allocates a task to the old people. To be particularly critical or prophetic is not to be expected of them. Carrying burdens, making plans, and effecting changes like the strong middle generation cannot be expected of senior citizens. They have earned the right to hand over businesses and leadership and to turn to something new: dreaming. This is what the Prophet says, and Peter takes up the idea when he describes the activity of the Holy Spirit and wishes it as a gift for the Church for all time.

This complementary relationship between the generations could produce interesting conversations today, because it shows what each one has to offer: different but of equal value.

The contribution of youth is considerable. Are young people today still interested in criticizing us, the Church, the ruling powers? Or are they walking silently away? Where there is still conflict, the fire is burning and the Holy Spirit is at work. In the search for Church workers and religious vocations, we should perhaps take particular notice of the difficult types, and ask whether or not these critics have it in them to become, firstly, leaders and later, dreamers. By this I mean leaders who lead the Church and society into a more just future, and "dreamers" who keep us open to the surprises of the Holy Spirit, who give us courage and allow us to believe in peace when battle lines are fixed.

You now belong to the older generation. What dreams of the Church do you have?

The Prophet reminds the old people that they are to pass on their dreams and not the disappointments of their lives. I am happy that today, here in Jerusalem, I can dream, like Jacob who saw the angels going up and down the ladder to heaven. Today I meet many people from around the world and from different religions. Among them are the angels we are allowed to meet down here on earth.

Once I used to have dreams for the Church; of a Church who goes her way in poverty and humility; of a Church independent of the powers of this world. I would dream that mistrust would be wiped out. I would dream of a Church giving space to people who think outside the box; of a Church that gives courage, especially to those who feel small or sinful; I dreamed of a young Church.

Today I no longer have these dreams. At seventy-five I decided to pray for the Church. I am looking to the future. When the Reign of God arrives, what will it look like? How will I meet Christ the Risen One after my death? I have always been an admirer of Teilhard de Chardin, who sees the world moving toward the great endpoint where God is all in all. His utopia is a unity, allowing everyone his or her own place, transparent and accepted by everyone else. What is personal remains, but we are one in God. The utopia is important, because only when you have a vision does the spirit rise above petty differences.

Is there anything that gives you concern among young people? Or do you agree with everything?

Quite honestly, what concerns me is a lack of courage. Certainly there are a lot of positives: many are studying theology today, and interest in the Bible has never been as great as it is in the Catholic Church today. There are also many social movements. I don't know that we were so perceptive of injustices in our youth and childhood as many young people are today. They are working for the homeless, for street children; they are going to South America and India to help the very poorest. This readiness to help is astonishing. Young people also have little hesitation in making contact with foreigners, other religions and churches. These observations give me great hope. And yet I am not completely happy. Fewer great experiences were available to my generation; perhaps in our case war and poverty prevented or even replaced those experiences. However, many of us followed through on our experiences, and made decisions. I was one of those, entering the novitiate of the Jesuits. Filled with enthusiasm, we wanted to give our lives completely to the service of God. We wanted to serve the Church and do many things better than the older generation had done.

Why is it that today, in an age of freedom and affluence, there is less and less criticism and only rarely major decisions? I find myself thinking of Jesus and the rich young man. Jesus saw him as an ideal candidate for discipleship; he sought to recruit him and praised him. Yet the rich young man could not follow this path and went away sad. Jesus did not reproach him or judge him, but it must have hurt him not to be able to win over this young man as a co-worker and make him an apostle. That is the same problem in today's Church. Especially on these questions that trouble me, I look for conversations with young people. They are the only ones who can give us the answer and show the Church whether, and how, our religious orders can survive and, above all, who in the future will look after the parishes, the schools, and the social institutions of the Church. By that I don't mean the many good staff and lay people who already carry the Church today; I mean the few who are needed so that a great undertaking, or the Church, can survive.

What I would like to say to youth and to the Church is this: *Have courage! Take risks! Risk your life.* Who should be putting their lives in the balance if not those who are rooted in God! I love the little word Amen, a word that contains our whole faith and praying in four letters. It comes from the Hebrew and, when translated, means roughly: I trust, I believe, I am secure.

From young people you expect more courage, more confidence.
Can a bishop be a risk-taker?

Of course a bishop must be more cautious than a young person; he must weigh up his words more carefully and consider his decisions more precisely. However, I hope to have risked a little here and there. Against all kinds of resistance and warnings, I met with terrorists of the Red Brigades in prison. I listened to them, looked them in the face, and prayed for them. I have even baptized children of terrorists, twins who had been conceived during the trial.

The terrorists came to trust me, and as a result something surprising happened: One day I received boxes full of weapons. They came from terrorists who wanted to give up the bloody fighting. Those in prison had passed on the message to their colleagues in the secret cells outside. The boxes of weapons were a sign that terrorism in Italy was coming to an end.

I still have friendly contacts from this time, and from the children I baptized good young people have emerged.

Have you personally never been afraid of making
wrong decisions?

Certainly some decisions I made might be reconsidered. If you ask my opinion, however, then a wrong decision is better than no decision at all. And again back to young people: It is just a matter of jumping into the water, particularly since many have the highest qualifications. We are rich, we are safeguarded, and many young people have a good education. But you can miss out on life for fear of making decisions. Whoever makes a wrong decision hastily or carelessly will be helped by God to make it right. I am not so afraid of people leaving the Church or someone giving up a Church position. I find it more depressing when people don't think, when they let themselves be led. I want thinking people. That is the most important thing. Only then comes the question whether they are believers or nonbelievers. Whoever is thoughtful will be guided. I really believe that.

How can we, how can the Church, foster in young people the courage to make decisions?

Perhaps our closeness and our friendship with them should be stronger and without any conditions. Of course some officials or bishops of the Church in our Western countries are still sitting behind walls that are too thick, either in new offices or in old palaces. When I see what a sleeping bag means to youngsters and how they travel, it reminds me of the begging experiment we did in our novitiate, and which our novices still do today. They set off on a pilgrimage, at least for a certain time. I often meet them here in the Holy Land. Young people go into the desert and accept a lot of discomfort. Just as Jesus recommended: take nothing with you, no purse, no food, and no second shirt. These words are at the very least a challenge to the Church to try some experiments with the simple life, with less bureaucracy. What about house visits? Who is game to speak to people directly? We would probably have more success in missionary endeavors and making new contacts if we used simple methods rather than having a full diary and official office hours.

Living in affluence affords young people many possibilities, more than my generation had. The more possibilities on offer, the harder are the decisions. I would like to give younger people courage to choose and not to wait too long. Not to make a decision is to miss out on life. That is the greatest danger today. On the other hand, the risk of making a wrong decision that needs to be corrected is a much smaller risk.

Anyone who has courage makes mistakes. But more importantly, only the courageous change the world for the better.

Genuine friends are given to the courageous. They learn that power comes from God's hands.

What is the source of your strength and your courage?

During my life I have had a great advantage, because the Bible and the languages of the Bible have been my life's work. Apart from all the scholarly work with the Bible, I think the Gospel is the richest source of creative material for someone who has responsibility for others. That goes not just for youth leaders, but also for a mother and a father, as well as all who are engaged in working for others. I also know business executives who read the Holy Scriptures daily, to draw from them ideas, strength, and comfort. I didn't need to have studied theology to have the treasures of the Scriptures opened to me. It only needs the courage to begin. Then you get the taste for it. It is easier if you are not alone, if you are reading and listening with others. I strongly recommend a pause after hearing the word. In that quiet space an answer comes to every listener. Perhaps questions will come up. I trust fully in the listening heart. Jesus enters it, even today. If you are seeking entry to the Bible on your own, you should preferably set out a program: each day at a particular time reserve a few minutes; or each week look at the Gospel for the Sunday, or even learn it by heart; or read the Bible from beginning to end; perhaps single words can be underlined or written out and questions and personal insights noted. From such initiatives Bible schools have arisen. The most famous is probably the one around Jesus. In Judaism this is an old tradition, and this very town of Jerusalem is still full of Bible schools. Questioners go to a teacher, to their rabbi, and study the Bible. Something like that could be important today, so that Christians might become independent.

Actually every Christian living with the Bible should find his or her own answers, in order to be a convincing witness for their faith in conversation with others. The parish and the wider Church would then become a surrounding framework, giving impetus and support; not a magisterium on which the Christian is dependent, and which he often uses as an excuse to leave the church. Leaders in the Church, including bishops, need strong and confident partners in dialog. It is probably the Bible that helps most in forming one's own views and a conscience and so making us strong.

Are there people in the Bible to whom you feel particularly close?

In times of anxiety I have sometimes thought of David. David experienced everything possible in a human life. He had friends. He sinned. He prayed. He was humble. He had respect and loyalty. He was daring.

Scarcely more than a child, he had to mind his family's sheep in Bethlehem. Perhaps in that he learned the most important thing for his life: to protect the weak, to lead the strong, and to hold them all together. He had to show courage. The prophet Samuel came to David's father to choose a new king from his eight sons. The father presented them all to him, except for little David, the youngest, who was out with the sheep. The prophet asked about the little one, whom the father had not even called. He was brought in and chosen as the next king. What would it have felt like for him to be given such a destiny and such a huge task? Perhaps he was helped by his own youthful lack of inhibitions. Soon he would be facing the Philistine enemies. Their giant leader Goliath was considered invincible. David wasn't afraid, and he conquered the super-powerful Goliath with his sling and with skill. From this time on he often had to do battle and show courage.

He was a servant to King Saul, whom he would succeed. The king suffered from depression, and David would cheer him with his zither-playing. He wrote poetry and played music, so that today many psalms still carry his name. David had to go into battle for the king, and he was successful—more successful than the king himself. People admired him, especially women. However, the king saw him as a competitor and became jealous. The king's son, Jonathan, saved David from Saul's evil plans.

Saul and his son were killed in a battle, and David wept for them. He was now king, conquered Jerusalem, and made it his own city. He freed the Holy of Holies, the Ark, from the hands of the enemy and brought it, dancing for joy, to Jerusalem. Now, all power was in his hands. One day he saw a beautiful woman on the roof terrace of a neighbor's house. He wanted to have her, and so he sent her husband to war, to a post where he was certain to be killed. He then took his wife Bathsheba for himself. Soon she bore him a son, but the child died in infancy. David was inconsolable. In his grief he became aware of his sin and the injustice of what he had done. He prayed: God, give me a new and steadfast spirit. The couple had a second son, Solomon, who became an even mightier and more splendid king than his father. David brought great kingdoms together and built the first altar to God in Jerusalem. Solomon later erected the temple there.

Despite all the external successes, fate dealt severe blows to the king in his family and among his own people. His son Absalom rose against him and forced him from the throne. David had to flee and was mocked. As he was crossing the Mount of Olives, the madman Schimi threw stones at him and cursed him. The royal refugee showed his greatness by suffering the disgrace and not retaliating.

After his loyal followers had restored David to the throne, he begged them to protect his son Absalom in battle, although Absalom had become David's enemy. The soldiers failed to do this, and David was again inconsolable. He returned to the gate of his palace and grieved there. His army chiefs had to force him to take up his reign again.

David acknowledged his personal guilt and repented. Moreover, he learned from his mistakes and defeats. What attracts me to this person is that he showed his greatest courage not in his successes, but in the way he bore the difficulties of life, enmities and abuse. He fought without thought of his wounds and dedicated his life to the task God had given him. David provides a fascinating role model for young people, but he could also give courage and inspiration to people in leadership roles.

Friendship is a central theme of the Bible. Can the people of the Bible become companions in life for us today?

Biblical friends have accompanied me my whole life. I think of John, the beloved disciple of Jesus. It might have been John who brought me to Milan and my charge as Archbishop. When the vacancy for Archbishop of Milan came up, many names were discussed, but no decision was made. Pope John Paul II had just read my book on John and might then have thought of appointing me to the position.

My book was about friendship. My underlying question was: How can we become friends of Jesus? In the answer to this question I see one single theme that can bring a young Christian to place his or her life at God's disposal. Not duty, not force, not even a situation of need can lead to such a life decision, but only love—a love such as the disciple John received from Jesus. John responded to his encounter with Jesus with friendship, with his life and his word, with the Gospel. And the Church today lives because of this witness. John and his brother James were among the first disciples called by Jesus. They left behind family, work, and even possessions and followed Jesus. That is a shining example of decisiveness without ifs and buts, a decisiveness of which only love is capable.

At first John and James were quarrelsome young men from an ambitious family. Their mother pushed for them to be allowed to sit on either side of Jesus. Jesus asked these young men, *Can you drink from the cup?* They answered naively and magnanimously, *We can!*—a healthy self-confidence that would only be tested and purified later in life. John belonged to the "three intimate friends of Jesus," as Albert Schweitzer writes. They were with him on the mountain when heaven was opened to them. They were the first to recognize who Jesus was and what he had to offer the world. And in the garden of Gethsemane at the foot of the Mount of Olives, they were with Jesus is his hour of struggle and fear. John was permitted to lean close to the heart of Jesus in the upper room during the Last Supper. He alone, on behalf of Peter, could ask, "Who will deliver you?" In the Gospel, John is the disciple who is described as "the one whom Jesus loved." He was privileged, perhaps even spoiled like some only children, but he was also ambitious and argumentative. John experienced and suffered times of confusion and fear; he stood at the foot of the cross, loyal and helpless with Jesus' mother, whom he was subsequently to care for. When Mary Magdalene reported to the disciples that Jesus had been taken away from the tomb, John raced there with Peter. He got there first; Peter was slower and, in his investigation of the empty tomb more thorough and precise. John "saw and believed" in youthful enthusiasm.

How does John see his friend Jesus? And what could we learn from his relationship with him?

It is interesting to see John and his character traits in comparison with the other disciples. John is the friend, Peter the leading figure, the rock, Nathanael the student, Thomas the critical one, Judas the tragic one, Andrew and James are the older ones, bringing the younger ones to Jesus. They all have different gifts and traits, and they are assigned different tasks by Jesus.

The disciple whom Jesus loved is regarded as the writer of St. John's Gospel. He knew how the other evangelists had described Jesus' life, and he wrote a completely different gospel. Through his love he was able to see more deeply. He had a unique insight into the heart of Jesus and gave us an account of what moved Jesus in the depth of his being. He courageously chose a free and artistic literary form to allow Jesus' deepest concerns to shine through.

The Church today must look for burning hearts like that of John. From them can emanate fire and new things. The Second Vatican Council was convened, in the face of many fears, by a Pope who had taken the name of Jesus' friend. He was so inspired by Jesus that he went beyond all barriers and gave free rein to the Spirit that "blows where it will." His courage came out of love. My most fervent wish is that today there will be among our youth some individuals who feel this love, recognize it, and then risk a great decision.

The view by the evangelist Luke is different from that of John. What does this difference mean for us?

We live with the people of the Bible. They are our unseen friends. They won't leave us in peace if we are too comfortable or blind. Luke provokes; he is a leftist. He sympathizes with the sinners and oppressed. He supports the sick. Jesus gives back to the widow of Nain her own life and that of her child who had died. Luke's feeling for suffering is not surprising, since he was a doctor. He fixes his attention on Jesus the Savior. He tells of how he heals and goes after the lost. Out of this, Luke, the disciple of Jesus, creates self-assurance and confidence. With his Gospel and his Acts of the Apostles he inserts the social dimension into the records of the church. Hospitality, surprises from nonbelievers, learning from mistakes, and the curse of hard-heartedness; these things make Luke a teacher with access to the hearts of young people today.

So how does Luke describe this Jesus? There are many aspects that speak directly to young people: Jesus makes himself independent; his parents must let him go. In the desert he finds his teacher, who dares to criticize riches and the unjust king. In his own words Jesus is concerned about successful people: "Woe to you who are now satisfied…, who are now laughing…when everyone is praising you…."

God "casts down the mighty from their thrones and exalts the lowly. He fills the hungry with good things, and the rich he sends empty away," sings the young Mary. Whoever stands so strongly on the side of humble people must be a critic of the rich and powerful. This is where I am most astonished at Luke. He is radical in his message and yet does not hurt anyone. He elevates the poor and shows the rich a way to handle their wealth, so they can make others happy as well as themselves. Everyone understands his message.

Luke sympathizes with the Samaritans, who were the notorious heretics. He argues on their behalf, showing their fear and exclusion, and portrays the merciful Samaritan as a model for all. The merciful Samaritan sees the neighbor whom the priest overlooks.

Luke even finds something admirable in the dishonest judge. Make friends with the help of unjust Mammon, says Jesus. According to Luke, we have something to learn from the godless judge, the poor widow, and the taxman Zacchaeus. Luke is the only one to tell us how the Risen One meets the grieving disciples on the road to Emmaus. He listens to them and asks questions. Young people were on the road with Jesus without realizing it. Only in hindsight did they recognize Jesus, with whom they had been eating.

Jesus, as Luke depicts him, is on the side of people who have the courage to stand up against injustice. Luke pays more attention to the women who accompany Jesus. He describes how Jesus makes friends and seeks co-workers. To criticize with love is an art. To criticize in such a way that it does not humiliate the other, but rather makes him stronger, this is something Luke can do. He builds a bridge between rich and poor, so that they can share their gifts.

You say that courage is a virtue for Christians. You create this courage from the texts of Holy Scripture. Is that the support system for your life?

I used to be an enthusiastic mountain climber. If you want to climb up a steep face, you have to have at least three pitons (technical screws) in the rock. With them you can reach up higher and stretch to a fourth point.

If you have only one piton, you hang there helplessly on the rock face and can't move. Even two is not enough; only three are adequate. Such pitons for me are the texts of Holy Scripture. They change in the course of one's life. It is interesting to ask which three texts are important for me. Which were important earlier in life? Which are important now? Think of God, who leads Abraham out from his home into the unknown. God is patient; he lets the weeds grow with the wheat. Jesus entrusts his mother to the beloved disciple. Jesus enjoys the hospitality of Mary and Martha: one of them serves, the other listens to him. The seed falls among the thorns, onto the path, and onto good ground. (I think of this sometimes in my work.) Jesus says: I have not come to bring peace but the sword. That means that faith calls us to make a decision; it is not there for false comfort.

Faith confronts, and it can also lead to people separating, as they go different ways because of faith. We should always be asking ourselves: Which texts in the Bible sustain me? Which provoke me? Who are my closest companions?—David, John, Luke? Who is close to me today?

You like to speak about your friendship with Jesus.
However, what of your relationships with contemporaries,
with the people around you?

Relationships and friendships can evolve in quite different ways. For example, even when I was a young student I began to visit prisoners every week. I continued with that right into the time when I was Archbishop of Milan. As a bishop I was most aware of my vocation when I visited people in prison. It is an easy task because the heart of these people in need overflows. I have seen much evidence of God's work in prison. The prisoners are desperate for connections, for a visit, for encouragement, and very frequently for forgiveness. They fear for the loved ones they are separated from. They cannot help them. Will their loved ones remain faithful? Often the prisoners are drawn to intercessory prayer and faith in guardian angels. "I was in prison and you visited me." I have directly experienced these words spoken by Jesus. Prison visits became a source of inspiration for me. I would go home strengthened.

In your home country of Italy you are much loved.
For more than twenty years you were Archbishop of Milan.
Why, at the age of seventy-five, have you come to Jerusalem?

I first had this wish to live in Jerusalem as a ten-year-old child, when a Jesuit priest told us about it. Immediately after his conversion, Ignatius wanted to go to Jerusalem, and he always longed to go. Why didn't he want to go to Santiago de Compostela or to other great pilgrimage sites of his time? He wanted to see the footprints of Jesus. I have experienced this same longing. On the way to Jerusalem, I prayed the pilgrims' chants, Psalms 120 to 134. In the meantime, this has become second nature to me when I go up to Jerusalem. Then I say with my whole heart: "Pray for peace in Jerusalem! Whoever loves you will be hidden within you." "Since all are my brothers and friends I say: Peace be with you."

Every day at four o'clock in the morning, I open the window of my room and look onto the old city of Jerusalem. I see the Church of the Holy Sepulchre, which the Orthodox Christians call Anastasis, Church of the Resurrection. I look over to Mount Zion, to the Upper Room and the Room of the Gift of the Spirit. I see the Temple Square, with the Dome of the Rock and Al Aqsa Mosque, I look down into the Valley of Hinnom and beyond to the Mount of Olives. On clear days we can see from Jerusalem, out in the Judean desert, the Dead Sea and beyond Bethlehem the burial place of Herod. I am surrounded by biblical people and places that have been part of my work in biblical scholarship my whole life, but especially in preaching and in personal reflection. Now I am at home here; as it says in Psalm 87, "Every one is born in Zion."

In this city the Psalms are on my lips: "How beautiful is your dwelling place, Lord God of Hosts! My soul yearns and longs for the Temple of the Lord. My heart and my body praise him, the living God. Blessed are they who live in your house, and praise you all day long. Blessed are those who find their strength in you, as they prepare for their pilgrimage" (Ps. 84).

Jerusalem has been the home of Judaism since Abraham, Isaac, and Jacob. King David built the city and Solomon the first temple. In Jerusalem God touches the earth. Right up to the present day, Jews, Christians, and Muslims have been fighting over that place where God is so near. The closeness of God brings the opponent onto the scene, the confuser, the *diabolos*. The city of peace experiences hate. At first sight Jerusalem is not the city of ecumenism and religious dialog, but the city of argument. The unrest of the whole world is concentrated here, but so also is hope. And we find again and again here that working for peace is a painful process.

The message of Jerusalem is not one removed from the world, nor is it removed from life; it is very realistic. It was here that David took someone else's wife. David was pushed off the throne by his own son and persecuted. Abraham bound his son, Isaac, as an offering and took him up the mountain where the Temple stands today. Yet it was also here that God showed clearly that he did not want the offering of a child, but our dedication, so that children might live. In Jerusalem the prophets were mistreated. The prophet Jeremiah was held prisoner in a deep well. In Jerusalem Jesus gave his life for us. The *Via Dolorosa*—the Way of Suffering, which runs through the city—runs through the history of humankind right up to the present.

Jerusalem is the city of dedication (self-giving) and hope. By the giving of his son, God conquered sin and death in humankind. The message of this city is that the light is stronger than the darkness. From Jerusalem the power of the spirit goes out into the whole world. On the Mount of Olives Jesus prayed and sweated blood, in solidarity with all people in fear and suffering. On the Mount of Olives Muslims and Christians alike have always worshipped the shrine of the Ascension of Jesus. We make a common confession that God raises us up with Jesus. Humanity is called to strive for higher things, and in all humility to lift our eyes to heaven. The Ascension tells all people that the judgment of history will be given from above. The heavenly

Jerusalem is our future, and it bathes all difficulties along the way in the light of hope. All things, great and small, acquire a heavenly dynamism. Jerusalem is an image of faith with all its difficulties. And yet, hope is stronger.

Jerusalem is my home. Before my eternal home.

4

Being Close to God

What is a Jesuit? Are the Jesuits strict? Are they left-thinking? Do they only take clever people? Are they pious? Do all Jesuits have something in common? I would like to know the secret of the Jesuits.

You must surely owe your religious life to a religious childhood home. If you look back over your life, what is the core of your spirituality?

My mother was a person of great faith, but without being overly pious. My father was less religious, but he was a very conscientious, sincere man.

To my parents I owe my religious roots as well as respect for people whose beliefs differ from mine. Through contact with other religions I have also come to know many good things, and especially many good people. To seek God, to be honest and ready to give ourselves to God, this is much more important for me than embracing a particular religion and its external forms.

In the "Contemplation of the Attainment of Love," Saint Ignatius teaches us a prayer that I say every day. It has become my favorite prayer:

Take and receive all my freedom, my memory, my reason and my whole will. All my possessions and my property. You gave them to me; to you, Lord, I give them back. Everything is yours; do with it according to your will. Give me your love and grace, that is sufficient for me.

How did you get the idea of becoming a Jesuit?

As a nine-year-old I came to the *Istituto Sociale* in Turin, a Jesuit school in my home city of Turin. I met Jesuits there who were very sincere. They said what they thought, and they put their love into practice. They were active for and dedicated to youngsters. Of course, not all people in the Church are so sincere, but we can leave them to the good Lord's judgment. Anyone who has lived and worked in the Church for as long as

I have has naturally had to deal with many difficult people. In spite of all the problems, I prefer to concentrate on the many fellow Jesuits to whom I owe my happy times and years.

What fascinated you about this order?

Ever since my parents sent me to a Jesuit school, I have never lost my attachment to this order. From the beginning I had good educators and teachers. Many were strict, but most were totally supportive. Their personalities and their dedication impressed me when I was young, much more than their weaknesses, which, of course, we also observed.

Certainly I was also attracted by the fact that education plays a major role in the Jesuit order. In the first place, with us a student is allowed to pursue a long and solid course of study, in philosophy, theology, and often also in another discipline. The studies always come back to the practical, particularly among young people and today in social action. For Ignatius Loyola, in his own life and in the founding of the order, the service of children and youth and their education was especially important, including the social aspect. In Rome he founded the Martha House for prostitutes and schools for the many widows and neglected children. It all began with their needs. Of course, Ignatius also knew how to obtain the resources and the political influence to make this possible. What fascinates me is that within his own lifetime, he was able to stir up in more than a thousand young people the heart and will to devote their whole life to the Society of Jesus.

The charisma of Ignatius—how can we find clues to it today? How can we bring it to life?

His attention to each individual and his courage to undertake large tasks, when he still had very few resources and brothers in the order, could be one clue.

Ignatius allowed himself to be touched by people and their needs; they made him a visionary. And he counted on God's power. "To act as though everything depends on you, and yet to know that everything depends on God;" out of this tension he drew sheer inexhaustible powers.

Again and again, popes entrusted the order with large, even overwhelming tasks; in more recent times it was dialog with atheism, today the conversation with Islam. One of the latest General Congregations placed the relationship of "Faith and Justice" in the foreground and set up many social actions and movements. The Jesuit Refugee Service was a particular concern of General Superior Arrupe, and today it is more relevant than ever. Also, for those suffering from AIDS there is a Jesuit network in Africa.

Father Georg, your work with street children corresponds exactly with our current commission. You began it at a time of need when the Iron Curtain fell. Without hesitation you reacted to a problem not previously known in Europe. I admire the young people's enthusiastic involvement.

The changes happening in Europe are an opportunity for the Society of Jesus. It has to go out and take risks. It must be courageous, or else it is not what Ignatius intended. He once said he would only be concerned about the order if it were no longer persecuted. The brothers asked him what he meant by that. He answered: "If we are no longer being an irritant, we have given up our mission."

Perhaps we lack this radicalism today. That could be one reason why young people are not finding the heart to commit themselves totally to the Jesuit life.

What is the task for Jesuits today?

We Jesuits should be helping people to find the meaning of life. We have the invitation from Jesus to be his friends, to live with him and to work with him. Whoever seeks poverty above riches, whoever can accept abuse and contempt rather than seeking worldly honor, who knows that difficulties can lead to a more mature humanity, this person is most valuable. Such an individual gains in confidence, knows why he is in the world, and has a glad heart. This fulfillment and his hope in what is still to come, these are the rewards Jesus gives. "Whoever will lose his life for my sake will gain it" (Matt 10:39b). We need to trust these words and base our lives on them.

Jesuits are familiar with a particular instrument in the spiritual life: the Exercises established by Saint Ignatius as a means of developing courage for decision-making. Could they be helpful for the laity also?

With the Exercises, Ignatius created for all people, and not only for his order, a method by which they can learn to be close to God and Jesus Christ, by which they can learn the discernment of spirits and make decisions based on their conscience. In the Exercises there are rules for making a sound and good choice. Today they have a new relevance.

With the Exercises, Ignatius showed Christians how, in direct relationship with God, they can become independent people capable of making their own judgments. And so, today, many young people still do the Exercises in preparation for making a life decision. They don't wish to be guided by an outside source or led by short-term interests through the next stage of their life, but rather, out of the depths of their being and in conversation with God, to come to a decision in which their whole life is at stake.

What is your personal experience with the Exercises?

Personally I became familiar with the Exercises as a boy at the Jesuit school I attended. I took part and was attracted to them, but it wasn't a real experience of the Exercises, because at that age and in a school situation, we couldn't do very much; and also because they were rather short. Normally they lasted only three days, and consisted simply of us spending some time each day for reflection and thinking about individual Bible stories. I experienced them in their full depth and meaning, as the so-called great Exercises, in the Jesuit novitiate. I did these for the second time in the last year of my formation in St. Andrä in Lavanttal in Austria. They lasted a full four weeks.

The great Exercises are a time of silence, a time every person has completely for himself. We novices came together only for common prayer; the rest of the time everyone was alone. Once a week we each met with the novice master for a personal reflection, to talk about how we had experienced the practices during the previous week.

The Exercises consist of four different topics, one "week" devoted to each. That does not necessarily mean seven days; a topic of the Exercises may take a longer or shorter time. It depends on the spiritual progress the individual has made.

How do the Exercises unfold?

The day begins with Mass. Then the person who gives the retreat introduces the daily program. He sets out points, each of which is to be reflected on for one hour. This meditation leads to prayer. Ignatius gives assistance for the hour of contemplation in the form of preparatory exercises. How much time I need for each of these preparatory exercises, whether I might spend the whole hour on just one of them, is left to the guidance of the Holy Spirit and the individual.

The first preparatory exercise is establishing the presence of God. I look up to God and seek a connection to him. A shortened form of this coming before God can be found in every major religion. In the Catholic Church we take the holy water, we make the sign of the cross, and we genuflect. When I have found my place of prayer, I look up to God in silence. This exercise creates an attitude in me. Ignatius described it in "Principle and Foundation," a text at the beginning of the Book of Exercises. It reads: "Man is born to praise God, to honor him and to serve him." In secular language: Man is called to something higher, he may look outwards and upwards beyond his everyday life and worldly cares. He has reason to be optimistic.

In the second preparatory exercise, the content for contemplation set by the Master of Exercises is recalled to mind. In the first week this subject matter is applied directly to one's own life. Ignatius requires one to deal with sin. There is nothing depressing about it, however; rather, it is a great release. I look at my weaknesses, my failures, my life story, and by so doing I also discover how fortunate I have been, that life today is so good. The aim of contemplating my sins is to realize how richly I have been blessed, how much companionship and help I have had. That broadens my view; I don't remain stuck with my weaknesses.

In the second week, at some stage in the Exercises we look carefully at a story from the Gospel. The leader of the Exercises gives an interpretation and preparation for the meditation. In this week we go through issues where we can personally make a decision. I ask Jesus to call me as one of his followers. With the help of my imagination I unfold the biblical scene in my mind's eye. The aim of biblical contemplation is to follow Jesus more courageously and more faithfully.

In the second week we also learn the "Rules for Discernment of Spirits." These are aids given by Saint Ignatius for making a sound and meaningful choice for the future.

In the third and fourth weeks of the Exercises, knowing myself better now after the exercises of the first and second weeks, I come before Jesus and contemplate his suffering and resurrection. I share with him my needs and difficulties and receive from him also joy and optimism.

The first preparatory exercise was the coming before God, the second the contemplation of one's own life and the life of Jesus. The third preparatory exercise is a short prayer, asking for what I desire, says Ignatius. That means, after the second week, "that I know you better, Jesus, I love you more and I am following you more faithfully."

The exercise itself consists of looking, contemplating, meditating, and remaining still. I should, and I may, come before God and Jesus Christ with the questions and wishes that concern me, and work through my personal hopes in relation to them.

At the end of the exercise Ignatius gives us the commission to seek a personal conversation with either Jesus or the Heavenly Father, and to conclude this prayer with a formal prayer. He mentions the Lord's Prayer, the Ave Maria and the Anima Christi:

> Soul of Christ, sanctify me.
> Body of Christ, save me.
> Blood of Christ, intoxicate me.
> Water from Christ's side, wash me.
> Passion of Christ, strengthen me.
> O good Jesus, hear me.
> In your wounds, hide me.
> Let me never be separated from you.
> From the evil enemy, protect me.
> In my hour of death, call me.
> Call me to come to you
> To praise you with your saints
> In your kingdom eternally.

A Jesuit usually does eight-day Exercises once a year, and through this he also learns how to lead the Exercises for others. As already mentioned, they help not only Jesuits, but also many other people, to build a spiritual life, to find a personal practice of prayer, and to develop the ability to make decisions.

Whoever does the Exercises is led into a relationship with Jesus Christ. He learns to reflect on his own life before God and so increases his desire for prayer, for silence, and for the Bible.

The Exercises are a challenging instrument in the spiritual life; we must be perfectly clear about that. Another task and an art that comes from the Exercises is much more widely known and practiced, and that is spiritual companionship. People who have done the Exercises will afterward often look for a spiritual companion with whom they can talk regularly about their situation and their progress.

What is spiritual companionship? Where can it be helpful?

The question posed by a spiritual companion will always be first of all: "How has it been for you during the past week?" Then it will move to a conversation about the intentions and plans made at the beginning of the previous week and what happened to them in the course of the week; this will include the question of what I have learned and observed as a result. And so then I make new plans for the next period. It is about the details of my daily life, from the practice of prayer to arrangements for work and life in the family or the community, and then to those points that are troubling me and things I want to work on. No topic should be excluded.

My closest relationships have come out of this form of spiritual companionship—older priests who were my confessors, and equally those for whom I was permitted to be a companion. Friendships developed; a mutual self-giving.

I think such relationships are a great opportunity for the Church to win over young people and to make them into real apostles for Jesus.

The Exercises for youth are a variation of the original program of Exercises, an attempt to show young people, in just a few days, a way for them to achieve clarity and courage, to come before Jesus Christ and to be able to ask with a willing heart: Where do you need me? Where do you want to send me? I really hope all young Jesuits and also other priests continue to use this valuable instrument, to learn to use it in such a way that they become masters in the accompaniment of young people. It is pleasing that women and lay people are also taking up this practice today.

The Church needs nothing more urgently than such masters or companions who understand how to lead others into a relationship with God. It needs people who are able to release in others courage and generosity of spirit, so that they declare themselves ready for God's work and the service of humankind. Of course that presupposes, first of all, the discovery of their own talents.

That sounds like supervision, which has recently become so widespread in the business world and in psychology.

This increased recourse to supervision—or professional advice in relationship disputes—is welcome and of great help to many. It may sound presumptuous, but religious leaders, including the rabbis, the desert fathers, confessors, and particularly we Jesuits, can claim to have invented the original, which has been copied and become widespread in modern mediation. Basically, everyone needs a spiritual companion in decision-making situations or in special difficulties and challenges. Spiritual companions are friends in the Gospel sense, the ones who accompany you, ask questions, support you, never come between you and Jesus but rather foster that conversation. If the Church wants to be of service to youth and be more attractive to young people than it is at present in Western Europe, it will certainly have to train and put in place many spiritual companions. If we can offer this service to people, by our example and by our own spiritual practices as well, it will not be without effect. People to whom I am connected through spiritual practices or spiritual companionship have my utmost gratitude.

Are the Ignatian Exercises and spiritual companionship something elite? Or do they also apply to the "average Christian"?

We need to understand that Saint Ignatius intended the Exercises in their complete form for only a few, for those people who offer themselves completely for God's service. For the majority, the exercises of the first week are often sufficient—a review of one's life and contemplation of sin in order to find a new way ahead. This is the starting point for the "Exercises in daily life," which are being offered more and more. They seem to me a possible way for many people to find an entry into the spiritual life. It involves the participants meeting once a week for a conversation with the leader or companion; he gives an introduction for the times of contemplation that will take place daily during the following week.

The Exercises are not something highly intellectual or inaccessible to normal people. They are practical and simple exercises for keeping love alive. It is similar to family life, where, in the course of a long marriage, love is kept alive less by grand declarations than by the loving arrangements of the everyday; what happens at breakfast, how the house is set up, how much time and imagination one has for the other, how they greet and say good-bye to each other. In the same way, love for Jesus and closeness to God is kept alive by everyday actions. I cannot imagine my life without holy water; the Lord's Prayer is a part of the life of every Christian. Here we have many exercises that are easy and don't require much time, but that sustain a spiritual life and allow people's own resources to flow freely from the depths of their being.

5

Learning to Love

I have been with my boyfriend now for over two years. He is OK. Of course we argue, but actually we get on well together. However, sometimes I catch myself wondering whether there is someone who would suit me better. Will I be happy with him? How will I know if he is the man of my life?

Andrea

The Church still has the reputation of being against the body or removed from life. One example of that is the encyclical Humanae Vitae, *of which only the ban on the pill and contraception got through to the wider public.*

The question is whether this ban is still tenable in a world of the AIDS epidemic and modern medicine. In any case, because of it the Church has erected a barrier to youth.

This criticism has been coming at me for many years from all sides, even from serious scholars and politicians whenever they are seeking dialog with the Church. The saddest thing is that the encyclical carries some of the blame for the fact that many no longer take the Church seriously as a partner in dialog or as a teacher. In particular, young people in our Western countries rarely entertain the idea of turning to representatives of the Church in matters of family planning or sexuality. I admit that the encyclical *Humanae Vitae* has also unfortunately created negative responses. Many people have distanced themselves from the Church, and the Church from the people. Major damage has occurred.

Personal and physical relationships are an essential dimension of human life with which youth must come to terms. From puberty onwards, young people experience a great deal of turbulence in this area. Many major decisions include issues of sexuality, marriage, or remaining unmarried. There is a certain tragedy in the fact that the Church here is so far removed from those who are concerned and are seeking answers. The encyclical *Humanae Vitae* comes from the pen of Pope Paul VI. I knew him well and admired him. I had the privilege of leading him and his fellow clergy at the Vatican in the Ignatian Exercises; they were to be his last before his death in 1978. This Pope was able to listen, and he treated people with respect. In the encyclical he wanted to be respectful of human life. He explained his concern to his personal friends by making a comparison with language. One is forbidden to lie and yet sometimes it cannot be avoided; perhaps one must conceal the truth or cannot prevent a necessary lie from occurring. Moralists have to clarify where sin begins, especially in cases where there is a greater duty than the transmission of life.

I find it painful that the "birth control encyclical," as it is popularly called, has left such a negative impression of Pope Paul VI in public opinion. He took over responsibility for the Council from his predecessor, John XXIII, and continued its leadership with great care. His even-handed approach was responsible for the opening up of the Church, for which he was able to win over a large majority. And I cannot neglect to mention his great interest in the Bible. The encyclical raised many human aspects of sexuality in a helpful way. Today, however, we have a wider horizon in which to ask questions about sexuality. The needs of confessors and of young people deserve much more attention as well. We must not leave these people out in the cold. They have a right to guidelines or words of clarification on matters of the body, marriage, and the family. We are looking for a dignified way in which to speak about marriage, birth control, IVF and contraception.

I often hear from young people and from many confessors about worries and fears in these vital life issues. At the same time I am aware of a new culture of tenderness and a less inhibited approach to sexuality. In any case, these beginnings point toward a Christian way of living together.

How could the Church indicate a way forward for youth, and to youth, with a new message?

As early as 1964 a commission consisting of specialists in the realms of medicine, biology, sociology, psychology, and theology prepared a comprehensive report for Pope Paul VI on the topics that were later dealt with in *Humanae Vitae*. However, the Pope published the encyclical on his own, conscious of his duty and out of the deepest personal conviction. He deliberately withdrew the topic from the deliberations of the Council Fathers; in this area he wanted to accept full personal responsibility. Seen in the long term, this solitary decision was certainly not an auspicious basis for dealing with the topic of sexuality and family. His successor, John Paul II, a powerful personality, went on to apply it strictly. He wanted to leave no doubt; he is even supposed to have considered making a corresponding statement that would have had the claim of papal infallibility.

After the encyclical *Humanae Vitae*, the Austrian, German, and many other bishops issued concerned statements that pointed to a direction that we could promote today. The passing of almost forty years—as long as Israel's journey through the desert—could afford us a new perspective.

In what direction do you see this new approach leading? And how urgent are the new answers?

Let us open the Gospel and listen to the voice of Jesus. He calls us to self-giving. Whoever gives his life will gain it. Where is there someone who will give himself for the building up of others? That is the core question in our dealings with others, and this includes the realm of sexuality. If renunciation is called for, it can only be the result of love and dedication. I cannot command renunciation without showing how attractive the goal is. Love is worth renunciation.

I am firmly convinced that the Church leadership can show us a better way than *Humanae Vitae* has managed to do. The Church will regain credibility and competence. Consider how John Paul II brought new life to the relationship between the

Church and Judaism, and similarly between Church and science, because he spoke the unforgettable words acknowledging wrong, words that have an effect today, centuries after the unjust judgments on Galileo or Darwin. In matters concerning life and love, there is no way we can wait so long. It is a sign of greatness and self-confidence if someone can acknowledge the mistakes and limited vision of their past.

Let us assume that the Pope says "Sorry" and retracts Humanae Vitae. *One would still very much hope that the Church today would say something positive on the topic of sexuality.*

The Pope will probably not retract the encyclical, but he can write a new one and go even further. The wish that the Magisterium might say something positive on sexuality is justified. In the past the Church probably said too much about the sixth commandment. Sometimes silence would have been better.

Love touches people directly; they cannot be excluded from the search for an answer and a way ahead. Let us consider the episode in the Bible where the Pharisees drag an adulteress before Jesus and ask whether she should be stoned. Jesus doesn't answer the question, but he judges the Pharisees because they have treated the woman as an object and not listened to her. Moreover, the man concerned was not present. In any event, the Church should handle questions of sexuality and family life in such a way that the responsibility of those who are in love plays a significant and decisive role. Whatever the Church can say will have to be borne on many shoulders, by responsible Christians who want to be considerate in love. If I think of the AIDS problem (according to the UN around forty million people are HIV infected, most of them in Africa, and in 2006 it reported three million dead), then it involves not only medicine, but also politics and cooperative

Learning to Love

development agencies. If the Church can bring all these parties into conversation (because the Church asks questions and listens well), that would certainly be a positive initiative.

In the Vatican discussions have been taking place about the use of condoms, not least because the Pope is deeply concerned about the AIDS epidemic. Even if condoms were allowed for HIV-infected couples as a "lesser evil," that is probably not enough. This opinion has got me into arguments. I have become *Cardeal da camisinha*, so I was told by a priest from Brazil. It means something like "Cardinal of the Condoms." So I am sometimes portrayed in an unfavorable light, especially by a few newspapers.

What is your quite personal view on these issues of sexuality? As a theologian, can you give some guidelines?

For me, one thing is of fundamental importance: self-giving is the key to love. A person is called to reach above him- or herself. That means being there for others and being dependent on them. Self-giving is also relevant to transcendence. We can climb from one level to a higher level. This dynamic is inherent to marital love; it starts with the purely animal instinct and the reproduction of the species, but it has a goal. Transcendence goes beyond friendship and partnership, beyond the protection of the weak, beyond raising children and on to the kingdom of God. By self-giving, people open themselves to God. In all our physical encounters, we strive toward this goal. Having this goal in view is more important than asking whether this or that is permitted or is a sin. Sexuality has a dynamism that does not leave you satisfied with what you have achieved. You will destroy yourself and the relationship if you stay as you are. Paul is referring to transcendence in the encounter, the growth of physical and spiritual love, when he says that the body is not for immorality, but for Jesus Christ.

*When you see how young people live out their sexuality
today—how can the Church begin a conversation with them?
What should it regard as important? What should it
be dealing with?*

In comparison with my youth, the world looks completely
different today; at least it is more honest and more open. In times
past you could not, and rarely wanted to, talk about the topic of
sex; it was pushed away into the confession box and into the area
of guilt. That is not its primary place; it belongs there only sec-
ondarily, when there really is guilt and there are problems. Today
I see a great openness. In this mix of parents, sons and daugh-
ters, adults and children, I can see an opportunity for a healthy
and humane sexuality.

This begins with taking conscious responsibility for the
child. Can I bear the responsibility of bringing a child into the
world or not? Young people are thinking about this and talking
with people they trust. Today no bishop or priest is unaware of
the fact that physical intimacy before marriage is a fact. We have
to rethink this if we wish to protect the family and promote marital fidelity. Nothing will be gained by unrealistic positions or
prohibitions. I have learned from friends and acquaintances how
young people go on holidays together and sleep in the same
room. It has never occurred to anyone to hide this or to consider
it a problem. Should I be commenting on this? That is difficult.
I cannot understand everything, although I feel that here, perhaps, a new respect for one another, a mutual learning and a
strong generational togetherness is emerging. This benefits both
old and young and does not leave anyone unsupported in their
questions about love and loneliness. I will follow this development with good will, with interest, and with prayer.

I don't think this is the time or place to look for generally appli-
cable answers. I always remember a basic pastoral or psychological
principle: that answers fall on fertile ground only when a question

is already on the table, when I have previously observed or listened. Especially in these deeply human questions of love and physicality, it is not a matter of recipes but of paths that begin and continue among people. A famous doctor thought that many people have an "innocent ignorance" in this area. We cannot require perfect lives from our children and youth. They will gradually find their way. The paths cannot be prescribed from above, from desks and pulpits. The Church's leadership will be relieved of a burden if it listens and trusts dialog with youth. The critical thing is to encourage in individual Christians the ability to make judgments.

Finally, the Church can and must refer to the Bible. The Bible noticeably limits itself in statements on sexuality. With regard to the breakdown of a marriage, it takes a clear line. It is absolutely forbidden to interfere with another marriage. The Bible is also very clear with regard to violence against women. That is forbidden. Children and all vulnerable people are central for Jesus. By its treatment of them, a society will demonstrate how humane it is. Apart from these clear guidelines drawn by the Bible, we are cast back on our own responsibility and the discernment of spirits.

We must not overlook the fact that, in spite of everything, a positive development in the understanding of sexuality has taken place in the Church. Previously sexuality was seen as very limited, exclusively concerned with conception. Moral theologians have spoken of *finis primarius*, the primary goal of sex. Also in this area, the Second Vatican Council opened up a much wider horizon and deliberately ascribed equal significance to the partnership and the mutual love of the partners.

Does this liberal approach also apply to the topic of Church and homosexuality?

In my answer to this question, please allow me the restraint and discretion I ask of the Church in regard to matters of sex.

Among people I know there are homosexual couples, people who are highly regarded and public-minded. I have never been asked, and it would never occur to me, to judge them. The question is how we are to deal with this matter. If I know someone personally, it is easier for me to deal with it than if I have to speak for general positions on it. The Bible judges homosexuality with strong words. The background to this is the problematic practice in the ancient world, when men would have boys and male lovers along-side their families. Alexander the Great is a famous example. The Bible wants to protect the family, the wife, and the children's space.

In the Orthodox Church homosexuality is considered an abomination. In the Protestant Church it is treated more liber-ally; there are even homosexual couples in the ministry; they are allowed to minister, providing they don't promote homosexual-ity. We are aware of the crucial test in this matter within the Anglican Church. In Judaism, the Orthodox strongly forbid homosexuality; in Reform Judaism again there are particular synagogues for homosexuals.

We are seeking our way through this diversity. The deepest concern of the Holy Scriptures, however, is the protection of the family and a healthy space for children—something now seen among homosexual couples. As a result, I am already leaning toward a hierarchy of values in these matters and basically not towards equality. I have now said more than I should have said. Let us proceed together respectfully along our different paths, but we must not come to blows because of those different paths. I have already mentioned the boundaries drawn by the Bible.

In dealing with homosexuality, however, we in the Church must reproach ourselves for often being insensitive. I am thinking of a young person who struggled with his sexual orientation. This was a burden to him. He could not speak with anyone about it because he felt ashamed. He felt he would be rejected if he acknowledged his homosexual leanings. This young man became ill because we didn't help him. Very depressed, he went to a psychiatrist, where he found a listening ear and encouragement.

What must the Church learn from this?

The Church will have to work on a new culture of sexuality and relationships. It must also do this to help with a deeply ingrained problem: in Western countries every second or third marriage is ending in divorce. The suffering that results from this is incalculable. We shouldn't blame individuals. We could and should, however, develop a new culture that fosters affection and loyalty. It is only in such a world that children can be children and grow up happily.

This new culture also needs to incorporate criticism of the commercialization of sex, from advertising to pornography, which finds its way into every living room. The mystery of love is threatened by this; relationships lose their magic. In the past we would speak of reverence in our dealings with others and with our own body. During our novitiate formation we heard a great deal about reverence as a general virtue, including our dealings with one another, discretion, and keeping certain things private. Even if this word sounds old-fashioned, today it acquires a new, critical relevance. Reverence is relevant to sexuality and is directly connected to the dignity of the person. I would definitely like to throw this challenge up for consideration here.

Celibacy is often blamed for the wrongdoings of priests, as well as the abuse of children, as has been brought to light in so many cases in the last few years.

This is where topics that admittedly concern sexual matters, but must be seen as separate, are all lumped together. It is terrible when children are abused. It is especially terrible when priests are involved; people who teach and should protect children abuse them. They are wolves in sheep's clothing, they are ill. It is painful and yet the Church has to learn to come to terms with this problem, more openly and more honestly.

Celibacy is another matter. This lifestyle is extremely demanding and presupposes deep religiosity, a good community, and strong personalities, and above all the vocation to live a single life. Perhaps not all men called to be priests have this gift. The Church will have to think of some way to handle this. Increasing numbers of parishes are being entrusted to one priest, or dioceses are importing priests from foreign cultures. This is no long-term solution. The possibility of ordaining *viri probati*—experienced men, tried and tested in faith and in dealing with others—is worth discussing, in any case.

I am very aware of the observation that many people, particularly the young, are interested in the topic of celibacy, although it does not concern them personally. This demonstrates the power this symbol has, and how great the disappointment if it is not lived honestly. Then the credibility of the Christian message is at stake. People in religious orders can make their vow of celibacy independent of the priesthood; there is no compulsory celibacy. This form of life will continue to exist as a sign inspired by the Gospel, and it is especially valuable in a world that suffers from sexualization and is seeking a culture. The hurdle posed by celibacy gives me the opportunity to pray for my fellow priests and to encourage young people to take the risk of entering that state.

6

For an Open Church

The Pope has attacked Muslims, then he criticizes Protestants, and now the Latin Mass is coming back. Everything is heading in the same direction. It's too cramped for me. Probably for the good Lord as well.

René

The anti-women Church must not be surprised if people run away from it. We sing "at the brotherly meal"— where are the sisters? At the altar and in the Vatican— only men. Aren't men applying the Bible in a sexist way? Where are the women in the Bible? They are only revered as obedient servants.

Evelina

The Second Vatican Council proclaimed the opening up of the Church to the world. Today the doors appear to be closing again. The leadership and those remaining in the Church place more emphasis on inner restructuring than on outward moves.

There is certainly a tendency to retreat from the Council. Courage and energy are no longer as great as they were at the time of the Council and immediately afterward. Certainly some treasures were thrown overboard in that first period of liberation. As a result the Church experienced a weakening. The arguments following the Council also consumed a lot of energy. Despite this, the heated discussions were necessary. I remember controversial theologians like Karl Rahner, Pierre Teilhard de Chardin, Henri de Lubac, and also younger ones. They participated in the theological work of the Council and afterward carried it forward in their books and teaching posts. They had to contend with those who were anxious, and they wanted to rescue something from the new theological scholarship. I can well understand their thinking, when I recall how many priests left their office at this time, how fewer and fewer people were attending church, and how a spontaneous freedom in society and in the Church had arisen. It is understandable that bishops and conservative teachers, in particular, wanted to stem these signs of disintegration and to return to the good old times. Yet we must look forward. Even if every radical change demands sacrifice and exaggerations cannot be avoided, I believe in the long-term perspectives and the positive effectiveness of the Council. It applied itself courageously to the issues of the time. It entered into dialog with the modern world as it is, without timidly shutting itself off. In particular, the Council located the many forces for good in the world, those that pursue the same goal as our

Church, namely, to help people and to seek and honor the one God. The great religions, and of course the various Christian denominations, want nothing more than to give a direction to those who seek, to heal the wounded, to work for justice and for conditions that enable all children and young people to have a good education and a humane future. They want to proclaim belief in the one God in order to make every individual strong and self-confident, because each is created, called, and led by God. Within this single great concern of humankind we find many sisters and brothers in the world, among believers as well as nonbelievers.

In Milan I had established the *Cattedra*, the "Forum for Nonbelievers," in order to hear from them what they are contributing to save the world, and what they have to say to people. I will never forget a famous psychoanalyst who talked about the prayer of nonbelievers. I wanted to have thinking people. They were to play a part with their search for truth. I asked the nonbelievers where they found their ethical base. A famous journalist replied, "I don't know. I have had no reason to live or to serve, but I have done it. Why?" He was the most honest.

I often emphasized that for me the subject was the main thing, that the nonbelievers were the teachers in this Cattedra. They had some critical things to say to us, which led to the Church making corrections and especially brought about a widening of its horizon. They showed me some problems and injustices in my own diocese. They offered the gift of tolerance to young people and took away their fears, because we all saw that they were not enemies but shared fundamental goals with us and sometimes came up with better ideas and ways ahead than we had. Through this Cattedra many Catholics, and particularly critical young people from our ranks, gained a readiness for dialog and conversation about faith. Some discovered the treasures of their faith and the hurtful boundaries of the Church in these conversations with nonbelievers. There was no sign of enmity, but rather friendship. The most important thing is that fears and prejudices evaporated. Out of these conversations came also my correspondence with Umberto Eco, published under the descriptive title "What do you believe in if you don't believe?" If the Church wishes to be missionary, and that it must be today, if we look at the decreasing number of members, especially, however, if we remember the original commission of Jesus, "Go out into all the world and teach all nations," then that compels us to enter into conversation with all people, to offer them all our friendship, and to try to work together with everyone. Then we will find common concerns, we will listen to each other attentively and learn from each other. Otherwise it is inconceivable how the Church can bring her treasures and the Good News to the world if these human connections are not taken up and nurtured. An identifying feature of a Christian is one who enters courageously into contact with people who think differently, people of other faiths, questioners and searchers.

In this opening up to strangers—in Jesus' time it was the Gentiles and the Roman soldiers—Jesus is our master. He was amazed at the faith of the Gentile centurion. He even judged it to be greater than the faith of his own people. He was astonished at the Gentile woman, who, even more than those in his closest surroundings, expected healing from him. Jesus conducted important conversations with councilors who were members of a governing body, the Sanhedrin. They were critical and dismissive of him. Also, his friendship with Joseph of Arimathea—who made his tomb available to him, and together with Nicodemus attended to the anointing and burial of his body—shows how Jesus was friends with people who were different from him. It is not by chance that the criminal crucified on his right and the Roman centurion at the foot of the cross are powerful witnesses for the significance of Jesus. These two set their hope on Jesus.

This was a program for Jesus that the apostle Paul later carried into the world courageously and actively. Here, too, we must not forget the arguments that this caused among the apostles, and the difficulties that the gospel of Jesus and the very early Church had to overcome. Compared with these, the arguments after the Second Vatican Council look quite mild. The fact that the Church flourished and spread we owe to the courage of the apostles at that time, and we need the same courage today; courage not to give in to difficulties, but instead to go forward and remain in conversation with everyone.

More than a few modern women are critical of the Church because of its rule by men. The invisibility of women, associating women with sin—these are key phrases. As someone who has spent your life working and living with the Bible, what do you say to this?

The Bible can help us in this, although some colleagues, men and women, even apply the feminist accusation to the Bible itself. They say the Bible is written by men, and because of this, men are in the foreground in the narratives and women in the background. That is, of course, the case; those times were different. And yet women in the Bible deserve more attention that they have had to date. It requires great care and attention to appreciate fully the evidence of women in the Bible. In fact, mistakes were made, probably by men, when Mary Magdalene, for example, was degraded to a sinner or prostitute, although there is nothing in the text to indicate that. There is a sinful woman whose name we don't know, who covered the feet of Jesus with her tears, kissed and anointed them. It is not Mary Magdalene. Making her a sinner is not justified. She may have been troubled or had a mental illness—"possessed by seven demons" is the biblical phrase. Jesus healed her. From this arose a deep relationship between her and Jesus. We meet Mary Magdalene among the innermost circle of women around Jesus. With his mother she remains faithful to him at the foot of the cross, she is the first person to meet the risen Jesus, he addresses her by name, Miriam, and she answers lovingly and reverently with *Rabuni*, which is more familiar than Rabbi, Teacher. It is a loving relationship full of beauty and faithfulness, a healing and strengthening relationship, radiant and open to the community, in which Mary Magdalene was a central figure after Jesus had been taken into heaven. I can understand that novels and films to the present day try to scandalize this intimate relationship. Sometimes human desires and fantasies are added. What we know and what I believe is that Mary Magdalene is the model believer. Because she loves to excess. Not moderately, not rationally, but completely. Through healing and friendship, Jesus opened her eyes to love. Mary Magdalene was a sensitive woman. There is excess in good as well as evil. Mary Magdalene stands for love, to which Christians are called, fully and boundlessly within the Good. To Jesus she was a fully human person. We should all seek out such people and be grateful for them when we find them. I think of the women of prayer who are the strongest force in the Church, and also of the women who work in the Church, who—I admit —are often behind the men. I look hopefully at the women, who always appear more self-assured in the Church, in the parishes, and in our society. Women have been partners from the very beginning: God created humanity as man and woman. The men of the Church must ask forgiveness of the women for many things; especially today, however, they must see them more as partners. In recent years women have struggled a lot; a certain feminism is necessary. For this reason men should not be fearful and allow themselves to become the opposite. Women want men, not "softies," I was told by an impetuous lady with astonishing frankness. With regard to the Church leadership, however, I would like to ask for patience. It will discover more and more of women's possibilities. Things have progressed a lot and will continue to progress, especially if we treat one another as partners. I invite you to take into account that the various churches move at different speeds in this matter. Our Church is a little hesitant.

Mary, the mother of Jesus, ought to be loved more by people today. To no person has God assigned a greater significance for the Messiah than to this woman. If we look at the Messiah's family tree, we notice exceptional women that the Holy Scriptures make to be links in the chain to which God attaches the family of the Messiah. There we also discover women who have unusual roles, impressive courage, and a good deal of liberating imagination. The Bible makes women strong and helps the Church to go forward.

In what way is it going forward? And where to?

It is noticeable that women everywhere are entering positions of leadership in the Church. Admittedly, this welcome development is born more of necessity than from clerical conviction, but it is a hopeful development. Leadership by women in church communities is biblical; I am thinking of Lydia in Philippi and the many women who were co-workers with Paul, who led his communities. In the New Testament we meet the deaconesses who were part of the early church until the Middle Ages. Women theologians have discovered the importance of these women for the Church in recent years.

Concerning the priesthood, we must take into account the ecumenical dialog with the Orthodox Church, and ways of thinking in the East and on other continents.

In Canterbury during the nineties, I visited Archbishop Dr. George Leonard Carey, then Primate of the Church of England. His church was suffering tensions because of the ordination of women. I tried to give him courage to take a risk that could also help us treat women more fairly and understand how things might develop further. We should not be unhappy that the Protestant and Anglican Churches ordain women and are thereby introducing something important into the arena of wider ecumenism. Nor is it a reason for standardizing the various traditions.

You want an open Church. You have the courage to take risks. What is your confidence based on?

Yes, I want an open Church, a Church whose doors are open to youth, a Church whose sights are set on the long-range view. The Church will not become attractive by conforming and making lukewarm offerings. I trust the radical word of Jesus that we need to translate into our world: as help for living, as the Good News Jesus wants to offer. Translating does not mean playing down. Jesus' word should show its impact today through our lives, lived with the courage to listen and state our beliefs. Jesus wants to give relief to those who are troubled and burdened, to point out to the rich the possibilities they possess, and to confront the unjust.

I am struck by the fact that Jesus asks: *Will the Son of Man, when he returns, find faith?* He doesn't ask: *Will I find a great and well-organized Church?* He will also value a small, simple Church that has a strong faith and acts accordingly. We must not make ourselves dependent on numbers and successes. We will then be much freer to follow the call of Jesus.

Often in my time as bishop I have reflected on the new church movements, many of which originated in Milan. I have wrestled with the question of whether they will lead us into the future. And naturally I have also asked myself, "Are they not putting normal, good Catholics in the shade?"

As a bishop you must have made many decisions with
consequences for the future. What are the criteria for
a good and lasting decision?

The decisive thing is that we listen to the Holy Spirit, that we
ask God as well as our brothers and sisters. Together with them
we can develop a program for the future. It doesn't work when
a bishop starts out with his own view and implements it. An
essential gift is the courage to stand up for one's own beliefs, and
the courage to speak the truth. It is important to recognize the
right moment for that. The Holy Spirit gives this awareness. We
cannot always proclaim the truth loudly. It requires love and sensitivity. Bishops are not alone; they can listen to their brothers
and sisters, their fellow laborers in the Church.

The Church always needs reforms. The power to reform must
come from within. Not only an individual, but also the community and the local church can do spiritual exercises, and reflect
on their journey, their successes, and also their sins. It can observe
the path Jesus took and allow itself to be led by him, to be
shaped by death and resurrection. From that will come the ability to deal with the future, and from there also comes the answer
to the question of how and where we are needed in the world,
where Jesus wants us to serve him.

Martin Luther was a great reformer. Most important is probably his love of the Holy Scriptures, out of which he created
good ideas. I personally owe a lot to the great Protestant authors
of biblical scholarship. In Luther's case, I have a problem with
the fact that he makes a separate system out of necessary reforms
and ideals. In the Second Vatican Council, the Catholic Church
also allowed itself to be inspired by Luther's reforms, and set in
motion a renewal process from within. The treasures of the Bible
were opened to Catholics for the first time on a broad basis. We
acquired a new relationship to the world, to its difficulties and

its knowledge base. Another consequence of the reforms is the ecumenical movement.

The fall of the Iron Curtain also brought change into church life. The Spirit blows like the East wind and the West wind. Do you see a new beginning?

A bishop from Eastern Europe once profusely thanked our diocese for everything that Caritas has done for his country after the opening of the Iron Curtain. The sentence he added has stayed with me: "We have received much that is good; however, we would prefer not to adopt the immorality of the West." He mentioned as an example that in his diocese queues of people stand in front of confessionals, and nobody goes to communion who had not immediately prior been to confession. In a few Western countries the significance of confession has been lost, he remarked. I had largely to agree with him. And yet I was defensive. I could only wish for him that the blessed times might last, and that he might withstand the materialism that is dawning over these new countries in the European Union. There is hope that these countries might learn from our mistakes. It doesn't have to happen as in a farmhouse in the Alps, where from one day to the next, the saying of the rosary in the evening was replaced by the television.

Complaining does not help, however. Pressure, morals, and duty have exhausted their powers, but what the Church offers is still in demand. More than ever, people are seeking relief and help through conversation. Today this need is filling the waiting rooms of psychologists and counselors. This is the domain of the Church; here is its great chance. It has a great tradition and competence in confession, in the area of discretion, of personal accompaniment and the gift of absolution. Today this offering is no longer self-evident; it must be explained. In confession one experiences the forgiveness of God. We cannot do that; it is grace.

Priests who understand the practice of spiritual accompaniment are sought after today. In the training of our people, more emphasis will need to be placed on this. I fear also that my fellow bishops in the East will have to change direction; away from being defensive and toward a search for new ideas. How are we to liberate the Church's practice of confession from the old ways of the ancient world and bring God's offer of pardon into the light?

"We must lead the way," Pope John Paul II liked to say; not whine or moralize, but discover and strengthen the good and the new, which means the Gospel, the Good News. This applies not only in personal conversation, but also in worship services and in preaching. Confession ends with the words, "I absolve you from your sins. Go in peace." That is an affirmation without "if" or "but," and without "you should." Jesus speaks in the indicative. "You are the light of the world. You are the salt of the Earth. Your sins are forgiven." When I meet young people, such an affirmation is easy for me. I see their happiness, their joy in life, their idealism, their abundance of ideas, their courage and artistic imagination. However, I also hear the justified criticism that youth directs at us. Anyone who looks at young people through the eyes of Jesus will experience surprising reactions.

Young people can learn from Jesus how to become evangelists, to discover and strengthen the positive in others. The Church needs this service from youth. Then people will again feel solid ground beneath their feet to support them. Their gaze will be turned to faith and not fixed on the negative. The Good News is the alternative path to moralizing.

In your eyes, what characterizes a Christian in the current situation?

A Christian is distinguished by his or her courage, courage that comes from faith. Christians know that God is leading and supporting them. In this very way God speaks through the mouths of others. It is therefore worth listening to the opinions of others too. Christians are not afraid of dialog; they seek cooperation with people who think differently and with those of other faiths, with questioners and the dissatisfied. With these people—in cooperation and in competition—Christians bring light into the world, orientation, healing, protection, peace, and the joy of living. Interfaith dialog and the cooperation of Christians in ecumenism will be required and accelerated by the needs of the world.

What might such cooperation look like? And where is its center?

In Palestinian Gaza, which is troubled by suffering and conflicts today, Dorotheos of Gaza lived in the sixth century. From him comes a well-known image of people of faith: "Imagine the world as a circle whose center is God and whose radii are humankind's various ways of life. When all who want to approach God go toward the center of the circle, they are coming closer to one another and to God. The more they approach God, the more they approach one another. And the closer they come to one another, the closer they come to God."

How do you see interfaith relationships? What are its goals? And examples?

Pope Benedict XVI has taken up the initiative of his predecessor, that of interfaith dialog and the common prayer of Assisi, in which, together with the great monotheistic religions, Buddhists and Hindus have also prayed. This was a courageous peace movement that came from the depths of the heart. In Naples in the fall of 2007 Benedict XVI resumed the dialog; the highest representatives of Judaism, Islam, and Christianity accepted the invitation, including the Patriarch of Constantinople and the Archbishop of Canterbury. It was an interfaith and international peace conference. That is a source of hope in a war-torn world.

I also observe the reverence with which the Dalai Lama is regarded among Christians; he receives invitations to Church congresses and from Christian politicians. With these invitations they risk their relationship with the world power China. The Dalai Lama has also visited me; he is a humble person. His personality challenges us to openness and peace. We can get to know the Eastern ways of spirituality, though perhaps not understand them. We must not imitate or mix traditions lightly. Young people value the tolerance and the reverence for all life forms—people, animals, and plants—that Buddhism has to offer. This also shines a light on the biblical teaching on creation. In the fall of 2007 I was personally deeply impressed by the protesting monks in Burma, thousands of young barefoot men, with shaven heads and in monks' habits, who demonstrated peacefully for freedom. They risked their lives for freedom and justice. Who among us today dares to offer his life so deliberately?

Mahatma Gandhi is also a great example for me; he never hid the fact that he derived his work for peace and his nonviolent protest from Jesus. He lived with the *Bhagavad Gita*, one of the central scriptures of Hinduism, and he valued highly Jesus' Sermon on the Mount. He was a strong fighter with words; he followed the path of a Hindu, the path to God, to whom Jesus leads us Christians.

The monks of Burma and Gandhi are remote examples.
Yet we have ecumenical problems close to us.

It helps to see our ecumenical tensions in the broad sweep of religions. Finally it comes down to the question, "Who will teach our youth to have faith? Who will show them a way to peace? Who will shine a light into their life? Who will make them strong to work for justice?" The development within Christianity is hopeful; ecumenism is sustained and practiced on the local level. Nonetheless, the Pope will always take account of the churches in the East, the Orthodox Churches, if he discusses with the Protestant churches questions about the priesthood, the ordination of women, and the acceptance of homosexuality.

In Europe, Islam is becoming an increasing political and religious challenge. What is the Church planning to do here with regard to Islam?

I think about Islam a great deal. I often speak with Rula Jebreal. She is the daughter of an Imam of the Al Aqsa-Mosque in Jerusalem as well as a journalist. She lives in Italy and is concerned with social matters. Recently she wrote a book about immigrants in Italy. Our essentially Christian countries have imported guest-workers and invited guests from Muslim countries. Over the years so many Muslims have come to live in Europe that we really have to look into the relationship between Islam and Christianity. This is an important and continuing question for world peace.

I see three major tasks: In the first place, we Christians have to let go of widespread prejudices and of the notion of all Muslims as the enemy. Terrorists cannot claim justification for action from the Qur'an. There are fundamentalists in both camps. Only education and social progress can do away with them. Herein lies a current task for us Christians: to fulfill our role as hosts, for example by helping in problems with schooling or language among guest-workers' children.

I am happy to see current developments in Christian religious education in which our children are being made familiar with the great religions. They will know that Muslims believe in the Virgin Mary and Jesus the Messiah, that they also honor the Christian Saints from the Byzantine era. Muslims bring their sick to Christian monks. They seek healing and help at the shrine of Mary in Ephesus. It is interesting to see how close the form of prayer in the mosque is to the Syrian liturgy.

Secondly, let us look at the differences between our religions. Arguments between Christians and Muslims have arisen from varying interpretations of the Trinity. We can find agreement between the teachings in the Bible and the Qur'an, just as Islam and Judaism have similar roots. The great medieval Jewish philosopher Maimonides was of the opinion that a Jew could become a Muslim at a time of persecution in order to protect himself, but not a Christian, because the Trinity stands in contradiction to his belief in one God. Clearly, for us Christians an ongoing challenge in our relationship to Islam is the belief in *one* God.

Thirdly, let us look at the practical aspect, the dialog between individual Muslims and Christians, the mutual hospitality and the courage to talk about religious questions. Should we invite Muslim friends to prayer in our church and go as guests to prayer at a mosque? Such dreams allow us to imagine that Islam is a daughter-religion of Christianity, just as Christianity is a daughter-religion of Judaism. The closeness of the monotheistic religions is tangible in the central biblical concept of justice; justice is the essential quality of God. At the Last Judgment, Jesus puts justice as the criterion for distinguishing between good and evil—action for the lowliest, for the hungry, the thirsty, the naked, the prisoners, the sick. The just person fights against social imbalances. The Qur'an calls the just person God-fearing. I would like to bring to the attention of Christians a text from the second Sura:

> Justice does not consist in facing East or West (during prayer), but that person is just who believes in Allah and

in the Last Day and in Angels and the Scriptures and the Prophets; he who gives lovingly from his possessions to relations, widows, the poor, pilgrims, to all who request help; he who frees prisoners, who prays, gives alms; who fulfills agreed contracts; who patiently bears suffering and misfortune and steadfastly survives all times of upheaval. Such people are just: they are truly God-fearing.

As a Catholic bishop, would you agree to the construction of a minaret and would you allow a female teacher to wear the veil?

The function of a minaret is to ensure that Muslims can be called to prayer. The question is, how many Muslims live in the parish and pray five times a day? If there are many or a majority, they will need the minaret, just as Christians need the church bells if they constitute a large group. However, Christians cannot demand church bells either, if they are only a small group among people of another faith.

The veil is a sign of declaring one's faith. I am not necessarily against it. Whether a female teacher or student should wear the veil at a school is a question for the state. Democracy will treat large religious communities equally.

7

Fighting Against Injustice

I wouldn't like to become like the older generation. They are only interested in money and their careers; they don't care about anything else. It's all the same to them if the environment is destroyed. For me, people are more important. I would rather live simply. I am against the exploitation of the poor; I would like things to move toward a fairer world. Who will have me?

Benjamin

What influence does faith have on politics?

As Christians we look to Jesus. He is the foundation for something quite new, the Church. Jesus took up God's commission to build a second tool for peace alongside the chosen people of Israel. Therefore he stands at the frontline. Jesus engaged in discussions with all the political authorities; with Herod, with Pilate, with the Sanhedrin, with the parties of the Pharisees and Sadducees. He became passionately involved for justice and wanted to change the world. The Church of Jesus Christ should contribute to making the world a more just and more peaceful place.

Justice, according to the Bible, is more than law and compassion; it is the fundamental characteristic of God. Justice means taking the side of the vulnerable and saving lives, fighting against injustice. Justice means being active and taking the offensive for a communal life in which all people live in peace. Justice must keep watch to see whether the law, as formulated, enables all people to have a good life. Jesus gave his life for justice. He therefore sought dialog with those in power—or they felt disturbed by him. Jesus put himself on the side of the poor, the suffering, sinners, Gentiles, strangers, the oppressed, the hungry, prisoners, the degraded, children, and women. Anyone who does this is an irritant. Whoever stands on the side of people who are like sheep without a shepherd, whoever gathers these people together and gives them confidence, such a person is a danger to the power holders. Even today, wherever Christians take up the option for the poor from Jesus, they must reckon with persecution. From liberation theologians in South America to social workers in affluent countries, all must come up against opposition, because they are acting from the conviction that meeting with the poor and fighting poverty is the privileged place for meeting God in our world.

Did Jesus have a political strategy?

"Render to Caesar the things that are Caesar's, and to God the things that are God's" (Matt 22:21). This is how Jesus answered the question about the division of powers. Cooperation between religious and state institutions, between humanitarian organizations, individual social enterprises and government organizations is important. We need all forces working until no one is left hungry.

Loving your enemy is characteristic of Jesus. The Jewish theologian Pinchas Lapide puts it better; he spoke with the highest regard of the "de-enemying love" of Jesus. Through this, the active, creative side so necessary for the peace process becomes clearer. If someone strikes you on one cheek, turn to him the other as well. That is: surprise your enemy and see what happens. A first move, a surprise, a generous reaction can sometimes cause hostility to collapse.

A look at the Sermon on the Mount is revealing. Whom does Jesus call blessed? Not the victors, but the persecuted. Not the happy, but the sad. Not the "haves," but the poor and hungry. Not the conformists, but the ill-treated. Jesus awakened the innermost strengths of the poor and made it a political issue. The political strategy of Jesus begins with him taking notice of people's needs. In fact, he lives with them. Jesus is asked for help by a great many people, and yet he doesn't give up, but seeks young people and trains them to be his helpers, to be apostles. This training of his disciples was, in fact, political. They learned what Jesus wanted specifically through the sharp exchanges that Jesus had, or was forced to have, with political opponents. Jesus turned the attention of his disciples to the needs of the Gentiles, who did not know God or the dignity of a person. His disciples were to go to those who were seeking help and allow them to experience the love of God, which is for all people.

The life of Jesus comes to a climax on the cross. He paid for his active involvement with his life. Perhaps one must give up success in order to have success. This is more than a clever strategy against evil. The giving of one's life is not easy to explain rationally. It is possible by trusting in *him*.

Is it reasonable to count on Church politics in matters of justice?

The late Pope John Paul II courageously led the way in Church politics. What he had to say on matters of peace, justice, and the preservation of creation was gratefully received on all sides, especially by socially engaged politicians. His invitation to the great prayers in Assisi was extended not only to representatives of the monotheistic religions, but also to Buddhists and Hindus, who were present and participated in prayer; this was a powerful contribution to world peace. It is no secret that this Pope played a significant role at the time of the collapse of the Iron Curtain. The suffering he felt with and for his home country did not break him; nor did he forget them, but through it all he became a strong fighter.

Within united Europe another front has appeared, the so-called "Battle of the Cultures." It is most noticeable in the confrontation between Christianity and Islam. In practical terms: How are we to deal with Muslims in Europe? Is religion a barrier between Europe and Turkey? Is the Church too accommodating or should it be more aggressive? Whatever happens, we must become better Christians. The outcome of discussions we can leave to the good Lord.

In our so-called Christian countries, the Church is still scarcely aware of these conflicts. Or are they not being noticed?

If they are not being noticed, that is a disturbing sign. The sin of the world—this is what John the Baptist calls the injustices he meets—assumes too friendly a face. This is a deceptive friendliness. The dangerous nature of sin is blurred. We have to uncover what is happening with the asylum seekers among us, how much time parents can give to their children, how little hope many young people have, how stressed both workers and highly paid people are; families often break up over these things. We must also take care not to get used to global sins; they are a challenge to us: the AIDS epidemic, environmental disasters, hunger, poverty, wars, and the terrible experiences of refugees, children who have no access to medicine and education, women who are ill-treated. Anyone who knows and loves a person suffering under such sins will be horrified and will want to do something. Here in Jerusalem I live in the midst of apparently insoluble conflicts among Christians, Jews, and Muslims. Here the confrontation among them is most keenly experienced. I try to maintain contacts on all sides and listen to their sufferings. Every day I pray for peace.

I often think of Saint Francis Xavier, who in his own times saw dreadful suffering in India. He wanted to go back to the lecture theatres of the Sorbonne and to shout: *Don't you see how great the need is, how much the world is crying out for your help?*

The sin of the world must not be trivialized or reduced to personal weaknesses. Sin is a call to make a decision. Who is ready to fight with Jesus against injustice? Who will go so far in this battle that he will accept, as Jesus did, disadvantage, humiliations, and sufferings? The world is crying out for courageous young people.

Isn't the individual powerless in the face of need and injustice in this world?

When I only follow a catastrophe on television or in the newspaper, I feel defeated and helpless. If I help someone, however, I am aware of my strength. Looking on is depressing, helping surprises you with the experience: I can save a life, I can reckon with the help and power of God. The first task of any social or charity organization is to create access for all people of good will, and first and foremost the young, to reach people and situations where they are needed. Building bridges like this is an art that people in today's social work occupations can develop still more. All young people have the right to be part of the fight against injustice.

What can young people do to show themselves trustworthy and become involved in working for justice?

I would rather turn the question around. Is it not rather we, the adults and the older generation, who need to win the trust of the young? Indeed young people are ahead of us on the path to justice. Who is making industry aware of the destruction of the environment, and making protests? Youth has a new and sensitive awareness of what we theologians call creation. We only need to be carried along by that.

I expect developments to originate mainly with youth. The year of social engagement, the daily good deed, radical Christian groups; all these have enormous potential. Sometimes there is just a glowing coal onto which we need blow to create fire.

Isn't it dangerous to use God's name in politics? Isn't it arrogant when parties call themselves Christian?

Everything good can be misused, even the highest Good. If aggressive wars are conducted in the name of God, if Christianity is used for populist purposes in an election, then alarm bells go off for me. Our Christianity proves itself first and foremost in just actions. In the Last Judgment, Jesus gives very concrete examples: feeding the hungry, clothing the naked, visiting the sick and those in prison, comforting the sad, welcoming strangers, and accepting all the difficulties that come with this, even to the point of being persecuted. It would be wonderful if others could recognize us as Christians because of such actions. On the other hand, it is horrifying when we speak of God and do not live up to his main characteristic, justice. With this view I also observe the discussion about whether the word *God* should be mentioned in the constitution of the European Union. If governments can argue their way to this statement of faith, they are bound to take an ecumenical approach, to be open to Muslims and also to Jews. Whenever God is spoken of, it must be taken seriously. Otherwise it is better not to mention God's name.

Could you give some guidance on how adults should engage with youth, so that Christianity can be passed on and can flourish anew?

Leave to your children a world that is not destroyed. Anchor them in the tradition, especially in the Bible. Read it with them. Have great faith in young people; they will solve the problems. Don't forget to set boundaries for children. They will learn to survive difficulties and humiliations if they value justice above everything.

themselves princes. He warned against surrender to "spiritual worldliness," settling into the comfortable life.

I read these words a week after returning from retreat, where I had read two superb books for priests: *Night Conversations With Cardinal Martini: The Relevance of the Church for Tomorrow* (Paulist Press. 136p $15.95), dialogues with Georg Sporschill, S.J., in Jerusalem in 2007, and *Notes from the Underground: The Spiritual Journey of a Secular Priest*, by the Rev. Donald Cozzens (Orbis. 210p $20). Cardinal Carlo Maria Martini, born in 1927, a Jesuit and longtime bishop of Milan, considered for the papacy during the previous election, had foreseen his recent death from Parkinson's disease and gave several

ON THE WEB
Joseph Hoover, S.J., talks about his new role as poetry editor.
americamagazine.org/podcast

church leadership the same way he and others had trained to climb mountains. They must enter foreign cultures, learn languages, stay fit with both sports and prayer. Cardinal Martini knows and loves young people well, having led thousands in Bible discussions in his cathedral; but he knows their weaknesses too. He worries about "the ones who are trapped in affluence, those who are bored, turn to drugs and sit alone in front of the television, who have never been invited to join a community. Some get involved in good works but "lack the courage to make a life decision." What would he say to them? *"Have courage! Take risks! Risk your life."*

Both Cardinal Martini and Father Cozzens hold friendship at the center of their lives. Cozzens, a popular author for priests, now a professor at John Carroll University, recalls that he had "power" for a while as diocesan vicar for clergy and seminary rector, and he remembers advice from a fellow priest-psychologist who reminded him that the clergy had two major repressions: sexual desire and ambition. Those who

DONALD COZZENS

order on Bea Fri 18 oct

800 258 5838 8 am – 4 pm Poy 914 745 0670

HAVE COURAGE! TAKE RISKS!

Two new books challenge priests and everyone.

Part of the excitement in those daily homilies Pope Francis has been delivering is that here is the pope saying things many of us have been saying to one another but have seldom if ever heard from the pulpit or read in the diocesan press. On June 20th the pope urged Jesuit journalists to attack hypocrites—intellectuals without talent, ethicists without goodness, bearers of mere museum beauty—wherever found.

I grew up in Trenton, NJ, sitting next to my father, editorial writer for the Trenton Times, at Mass while the pastor, who seems never to have prepared a sermon, snarled against the secular press, as if those words were obscene. And today some blame "threats" to the church on the press. Two days later Francis turned his words toward bishops who consider

very frank interviews, with the hope that those who loved and admired him during his life would act on the ideas they had discussed.

A few days before he died, he told Father Sporschill that "the church is 200 years behind the times." Why don't we rouse ourselves, are we afraid? "The church is tired in affluent Europe and America. Our culture has grown old, our churches are big, our religious houses are empty, the bureaucracy of our churches is growing out of proportion, our liturgies and our vestments are pompous. Yet maybe these things express what we've become today." He urged the pope and bishops to find 12 unconventional people to take on leadership roles, people close to the poor who can galvanize young people to take charge.

The young, he said, had to train for

Night Conversations
with Cardinal Martini
CARDINAL CARLO M. MARTINI AND GEORG SPORSCHILL
The Relevance of the Church for Tomorrow

NOTES FROM THE
UNDERGROUND
THE SPIRITUAL JOURNAL OF A SECULAR PRIEST